D0078297

Ann Petry

Twayne's United States Authors Series

Frank Day, Editor
Clemson University

TUSAS 667

ANN PETRY. PHOTOGRAPH BY CARL VAN VECHTEN, 1948.

From The Ann Petry Collection, Boston University Libraries.
Reprinted with permission of the Estate of Carl Van Vechten, Joseph Solomon, Executor.

Ann Petry

Hilary Holladay

University of Massachusetts, Lowell

Twayne Publishers
An Imprint of Simon & Schuster Macmillan
New York

Prentice Hall International
London • Mexico City • New Delhi • Singapore • Sydney • Toronto

Twayne's United States Authors Series No. 667

Ann Petry
Hilary Holladay

Copyright © 1996 by Twayne Publishers
All rights reserved. No part of this book may be reproduced or transmitted in any form or by any means, electronic or mechanical, including photocopying, recording, or by any information storage and retrieval system, without permission in writing from the Publisher.

Twayne Publishers
An Imprint of Simon & Schuster Macmillan
1633 Broadway
New York, New York 10019

Library of Congress Cataloging-in-Publication Data

Holladay, Hilary.
    Ann Petry / Hilary Holladay.
        p.   cm.—(Twayne's United States authors series ; TUSAS 667)
    Includes bibliographical references and index.
    ISBN 0-8057-7842-X
    1. Petry, Ann Lane, 1908–   —(Criticism and interpretation. 2. Women and literature—United States—History—20th century. 3. Afro-Americans in literature. 4. New England—In literature. I. Title. II. Series.
PS3531.E933Z69   1996
813'.54—dc20   96-15385
                                                                                              CIP

The paper used in this publication meets the minimum requirements of American National Standard for Information Sciences—Permanence of Paper for Printed Library Materials, ANSI Z39.48-1984. ∞™

10 9 8 7 6 5 4 3 2 1

Printed in the United States of America

PS
3531
,E933
Z69
1996

081296/2408 D2

In memory of my mother,
Catharine Mitchell Holladay

Contents

Chronology

1908   Ann Lane is born 12 October to Peter Clark Lane Jr. and Bertha James Lane in Old Saybrook, Connecticut, the younger of two daughters.

1925   Graduates from Old Saybrook High School.

1931   Earns Ph.G. degree from Connecticut College of Pharmacy in New Haven (now School of Pharmacy at the University of Connecticut, Storrs). Works in family drugstores in Old Saybrook and Old Lyme, Connecticut, until 1938.

1938   Marries George D. Petry of New Iberia, Louisiana, on 22 February. With husband, moves to New York City and works as advertising representative and journalist for *Amsterdam News* in Harlem until 1941.

1939   Using the pseudonym Arnold Petri, publishes first short story, "Marie of the Cabin Club," in the Baltimore *Afro-American.*

1940   Joins American Negro Theatre in New York. Plays Tillie Petunia in *On Striver's Row* at the Schomburg Center for Research in Black Culture.

1941   Employed as editor of woman's page and reporter for *People's Voice* in Harlem. Studies art at Harlem Art Center.

1942   Writes weekly column, "The Lighter Side," for *People's Voice* through 1943. Attends Mabel Louise Robinson's creative writing workshop at Columbia University through 1944. Helps found Negro Women, Inc., consumer protection organization in Harlem.

1943   Publishes "On Saturday the Siren Sounds at Noon" in the *Crisis.* On the basis of this story, Houghton Mifflin editor invites her to enter Houghton Mifflin Literary Fellowship competition.

1944   Submits opening chapters and an outline of *The Street* to Houghton Mifflin Literary Fellowship competition.

1945   Wins fellowship competition in fiction; receives stipend of $2,400.

1946   Publishes *The Street*. *The Best American Short Stories* (1946, edited by Martha Foley) is dedicated to Ann Petry. Includes Petry's "Like a Winding Sheet."

1947   Publishes *Country Place*. With her husband, purchases eighteenth-century home in Old Saybrook and moves there.

1949   Birth of daughter, Elisabeth Ann Petry. Death of father. Publishes first book for children, *The Drugstore Cat*.

1953   Publishes *The Narrows*.

1955   Publishes *Harriet Tubman, Conductor on the Underground Railroad*, for children.

1956   Death of mother.

1958   Works for Columbia Pictures, writing script for a Kim Novak vehicle, *That Hill Girl*.

1964   Publishes *Tituba of Salem Village*, for children.

1970   Publishes *Legends of the Saints*, for children.

1971   Publishes *Miss Muriel and Other Stories*, first collection of stories published by an African-American woman writer.

1974   Employed as visiting professor of English at the University of Hawaii.

1976   Publishes poems "Noo York City 1," "Noo York City 2," and "Noo York City 3" in *Weid: The Sensibility Revue* (Bicentennial Issue II, American Women Poets).

1981   Publishes poems "A Purely Black Stone" and "A Real Boss Black Cat" in *A View from the Top of the Mountain*.

1982   Delivers Fourth Annual Richard Wright Lecture, Yale University.

1983   Receives Doctor of Letters, Suffolk University.

1984   Receives award from Connecticut Historical Society, Black Women of Connecticut: Achievement against the Odds.

1985   Beacon Press reprints *The Street*. Petry is honored for literary achievements by City of Philadelphia.

1986   Publishes short story "The Moses Project" in *Harbor Review* (English Department, University of Massachusetts, Boston).

1988   Beacon Press reprints *The Narrows* and *The Drugstore Cat*. Petry receives Doctor of Letters from University of Connecticut and citation from United Nations Association of the United States of America.

1989   Beacon Press reprints *Miss Muriel and Other Stories*. Petry receives Doctor of Humane Letters from Mount Holyoke College and Lifetime Achievement Award during Fifth Annual Celebration of Black Writers Conference in Philadelphia.

1992   Houghton Mifflin reissues *The Street*. Petry receives Connecticut Arts Award from Connecticut Commission on the Arts in Stamford. Ann Petry Conference, a scholarly symposium, held 14 November at Trinity College in Hartford, Connecticut. As part of the conference, Petry attends "A Tribute to Ann Petry" by Gloria Naylor. Mayor of Hartford declares 14 November "Ann Petry Day." Petry reads excerpts from her writing as part of "Connecticut Voices" series on Connecticut Public Radio in Hartford (14 November).

Acknowledgments

I wish to thank Trudier Harris, Linda Wagner-Martin, and William H. Roberts for all of their guidance and encouragement. I also wish to thank the University of Massachusetts, Lowell, and the University of North Carolina at Chapel Hill for grants enabling me to complete my research.

Thanks also to Laura Terry Sellers, Elinor Ann Walker, and Keith S. Clark for their generous friendship during the writing of this book. And special thanks to my father, George R. Holladay, and my sisters, Julie Holladay Mann and Cary C. Holladay, for their sustaining love and support.

Two sections of this volume were originally published in slightly different form as essays: "Creative Prejudice in Ann Petry's 'Miss Muriel,'" *Studies in Short Fiction* 31 (1994), and "Narrative Space in Ann Petry's *Country Place*," *Xavier Review* 16, no. 1 (1996).

Chapter One
Ann Petry, Neighborhood Novelist

After the publication of Ann Petry's third novel, *The Narrows* (1953), Arna Bontemps declared her "a neighborhood novelist." He explained that "Just as some storytellers train their sights on a roomful of people, a nest of simple folk, a company of travellers, a town, a family, or an individual, Ann Petry elects the neighborhood as her unit."[1] Although the word "neighborhood" may evoke comforting images of people lounging on porches and children playing on the sidewalk, Petry's renditions of neighborhood life in *The Street* (1946), *Country Place* (1947), *The Narrows,* and *Miss Muriel and Other Stories* (1971) are far from comforting. In fact, her neighborhoods—that is, communities within larger communities— are often violently unhappy places. But more to the point, they are *living* places where people's sometimes destructive attitudes toward each other shape the neighborhood's overall identity. Rather than merely maligning the harmful effects of social prejudices, Petry shows how biases of race, gender, and age (to name just a few) influence the lives of all the neighborhood's residents, no matter whether they are old or young, male or female, white or nonwhite.

In Petry's framing of her own life, she emphasizes neighborhood experience as well.[2] Born 12 October 1908 to Peter Clark Lane Jr. (1872–1949), and Bertha James Lane (1875–1956), the younger of two daughters, Ann Lane did not grow up experiencing the poverty and desperation that afflicted many of the blacks she encountered as an adult in Harlem. But in her native Old Saybrook, Connecticut, a small resort town nearly surrounded by water, she quickly learned about the boundaries separating her family from the rest of their nearly all-white community. In an autobiographical essay, she recollects her decision at the age of four to start school along with her six-year-old sister, Helen. Their father expected that Ann would be sent home as soon as the teacher found out how old she was. But no one asked her age, so Ann, in pigtails and shiny new shoes, began her formal education two years ahead of schedule.

Her education quickly took a traumatic turn. On the way home that first day, white boys—older and bigger than their victims—chased and stoned the little girls. The Lane sisters ran home, frightened, crying, determined never to return to school. But their parents vetoed this plan. Peter and Bertha Lane insisted that the girls go back the next day. This time, they said, Ann and Helen wouldn't get hurt. Recollecting the events seventy-five years later, Ann Petry writes:

> And so—the next morning my mother walked to school with us. Nothing happened. She assured us that we could come home alone safely. We didn't quite believe her.
>
> Sure enough, as soon as we were out of sight of the school the same boys started to stone us. Two of our uncles appeared, quite suddenly, and started knocking the attackers down—some of them they held and knocked their heads together, as they threatened them with sudden and violent death. After that we walked home from school without incident. (*CAAS*, 256)

At four, Ann Lane heard the stinging words of racism and felt the stones that brought the message home. But her family, working together first behind the scenes and then out in the open, responded with a message that was equally clear: The Lane sisters would not be denied the right to walk calmly, learn diligently, or fight back ferociously in the world they shared with other children, grownups, strangers, people of all colors.

The episode was a defining moment in the life of Ann Lane Petry, African-American woman, New Englander, writer for adults and children. She used the germ of the experience in "Doby's Gone," the concluding story in *Miss Muriel and Other Stories*, the first short-fiction collection published by an African-American woman. Weaving the facts into an imaginative frame gave vent to the emotion she had felt for so long: "This story is in a way another expression of the outrage that has stayed with me all these years," she writes. "To paraphrase a sentence from one of James Baldwin's great essays, this sense of outrage stayed with me, 'indivisible from me forever, part of the passion that drives me'" (*CAAS*, 256).

Ann Petry's outrage, wrapped in a passion for storytelling, has driven her to write and publish eight books: the story collection, three novels, and four books for juvenile readers. "Having been born black and female, I regard myself as a survivor and a gambler, writing in a tradition that dates back to 1859 when *Our Nig,* the first novel written by a black woman [Harriet Wilson] in this country, was published in Boston,

Massachusetts," Petry observes (*CAAS*, 253). She goes on to elaborate on her self-definition:

> Like all writers, black or white, I work against odds, real or imaginary, against hostility, against indifference. I keep seeking uninterrupted time in which to write and so I wage war against interruptions. I am usually defeated by my archenemy the telephone or by people who do not regard writing as work and drop in to visit.
>
> I regard myself as a survivor because I have written eight books and had them published.
>
> I regard myself as a gambler because each one of these books was written against odds that it would ever be finished, enormous odds that only a gambler would have accepted. (*CAAS*, 253)

The characters in Petry's fiction also face imposing odds. While the subjects of her children's books are heroic figures like Harriet Tubman, who beat the odds, the characters in her adult fiction are not nearly so victorious. They often take risks, but they don't often succeed.

From New England Roots to Urban Streets

The Street, her best-selling first novel, is a painfully vivid portrait of the effects of racism and sexism on a young black woman, Lutie Johnson, in World War II Harlem. The narrative focuses mainly on Lutie, but it also enters the minds of her fellow tenement dwellers and her eight-year-old son. *Country Place* shifts location to a small New England town similar to Petry's native Old Saybrook. It concerns the claustrophobic, unhappy lives of the white families making up the community of Lennox. The white narrator, Doc, is a druggist who dryly records the occasions when the town's finest citizens get a taste of their own bitter medicine. *The Narrows* explores the themes of miscegenation and betrayal in an upstate New York town. The style of narration is similar to that of *The Street;* the story begins from the perspective of Abby Crunch, a middle-aged black woman, but later moves in and out of the minds of an array of black and white characters. *Miss Muriel and Other Stories* brings together thirteen works of short fiction representing three decades of Petry's writing career. As in her novels, the narrative voice in her stories is forthright and easy to listen to—a slippery guise for difficult subject matter. Some of the stories, like "Doby's Gone," spring from memorable events in Petry's childhood, while others, such as "The Witness" and "Like a

Winding Sheet," address the tangled issues of race, violence, and sexuality as they manifest themselves in the lives of adults.

The Walking Wounded

Ann Petry's fiction deals with prejudices of race, sex, and class and with the ways in which the American dream of success and plenitude haunts, and finally mocks, those people who fail to achieve it. She writes in rhythmic, deceptively simple prose, frequently underscoring the unsettled, disrupted nature of human relations via setting and environmental detail. Petry calls her characters "the walking wounded" (*CAAS*, 253), and her use of naturalism, especially in *The Street* and *Country Place,* provides them with realistically portrayed, yet fundamentally unstable, ground on which to make their hobbling way.

In 1950, Petry suggested why people want to read fiction that addresses difficult social issues:

> Possibly the reading public, and here I include myself, is like the man who kept butting his head against a stone wall and when asked for an explanation said that he went in for this strange practice because it felt so good when he stopped. Perhaps there is a streak of masochism in all of us; or perhaps we all feel guilty because of the shortcomings of society and our sense of guilt is partially assuaged when we are accused, in the printed pages of a novel, of having done those things that we ought not to have done—and of having left undone those things we ought to have done.[3]

Because racism and sexism and their consequences remain integral to life in America, Petry's characterizations of these prejudices in her fiction continue to inspire feelings of masochism and guilt. Although she did the bulk of her writing midcentury, her novels and stories articulate the same pain and outrage expressed by contemporary chroniclers of sexism and racism. Petry's works are thus more timeless—and timely—than one might like them to be. Petry herself has said of *The Street,* "It just saddens my heart so that if you added crack, it would basically be the same story today. It's just so painful and frightening."[4]

American Dream Come True

The great irony of Ann Petry's life is that despite being black and female she has achieved the American dream that so persistently eludes her characters. Although she sees herself as a gambler and survivor, she began life with advantages commonly associated with guaranteed prosperity, to say nothing of survival. A happy home, where poverty was not an issue, did not necessarily precipitate fame and fortune, of course, but it helped give her the self-confidence as a writer that belonging to an oppressed race and gender might otherwise have diminished—or erased entirely.

A fourth-generation native of Connecticut, Ann Lane was blessed from the start with ambitious, practical parents. Following in the tradition of his father, a chemist, Peter Lane Jr., became a pharmacist and opened his own drugstore in Old Saybrook in 1902. His enterprising wife, Bertha, was a "chiropodist, hairdresser, licensed barber, manufacturer of hair tonic, creator of a liquid cleaner for use in the bathroom, owner and creator of a thriving business in the creation of elegant embroidered and hemstitched linens" (*CAAS*, 260). The couple had many interests beyond their businesses. Petry reels off the other dimensions of her father's identity: "storyteller, tenor in the choir of the Congregational Church, fancy figure skater, expert swimmer, collector of old drug bottles, occasional gardener" (*CAAS*, 259). And her mother was "a dedicated gardener and a collector of antiques. Years before other people began to buy some of the old and rare things in the world she was buying them" (*CAAS*, 260). Her parents, then, were busy people who honed their professional skills and nurtured their natural talents. When they had their two children, after several years of trying, they were more than ready to pass on their enthusiasm and curiosity about the world.

Ann's birth added another powerful presence in a family of strong, well-loved women. When she was twelve, they moved out of the drugstore building because Bertha Lane wanted a home removed from the family business: "She bought a piece of land in another part of the town and had a house built on it, a house with a fireplace" (*CAAS*, 260). Bertha Lane's engineering of the move, along with her daughter's proud recounting of it, suggests that in this family women pursued and got what they wanted. The point is also illustrated by Ann's two impressively resourceful maternal aunts: one was a licensed pharmacist who eventually took over the family drugstore; another was a teacher who ran a correspondence course in reading and literature. In a 1992 interview with the *Washington Post,* Petry comments on the successful women in her family, noting that as far as she could tell, "it never occurred to them that there were things they couldn't do because they were women." And they attracted men who loved them for their strength: "I imagine if my mother or her sisters said, 'Lie down and let me walk on you,' these men probably would have—and said it felt good."[5]

A Family of Storytellers

But the men in the family were far from passive. Petry has fond memories not only of her loving, witty father but also of her well-traveled uncles, who entertained the whole family with tales of their adventures. Storytelling was, put simply, in the blood: "We always had relatives visiting us. They added excitement to our lives. They brought with them the aura and the customs of a very different world. They were all storytellers, spinners of yarns. So were my mother and my father" (*CAAS,* 257). The uncles, who were Bertha Lane's brothers, provided more than enough material for a future writer's percolating mind: "They had quite literally lived all over the world—in Africa, in Asia, in Europe. They had been roustabouts with circuses, seamen, pullman-car porters, longshoremen, butchers, barbers, waiters, bartenders. They had worked in factories. One of them had helped smuggle Chinese over the border between the United States and Canada" (*CAAS,* 257). Although there were few other blacks in Old Saybrook, the Lane children had the benefit of role models in their own close, high-spirited family. Ann and her sister were filled with ambitions that they might not have entertained had they lived in a city along with thousands of poor blacks stuck in demeaning jobs.

After beginning school two years early, Ann remained a precocious student, reading ahead in her assignments and devouring whatever literature came her way. She remembers the encouragement of certain teachers, especially an English teacher she didn't much care for. A test question required her to dream up a scene between two characters in *A Tale of Two Cities,* and Ann plunged into it with the fervor of one no longer worrying about grades. The teacher read her essay to the class the following Monday and announced that "'I honestly believe that you could be a writer if you wanted to'" (*CAAS,* 263). The memorable compliment came from an authority with no predilection for flattery; Petry now says, "The seed was sown by the praise of Caesar" (Fein, B2).

That seed was nurtured by $5 she received for writing a slogan for a perfume company. The sale was "a revelation—I could actually be paid for putting words on paper" (*CAAS,* 263). But Ann was not the girl-writer-prodigy that her fellow New Englander Sylvia Plath (1931–62) was destined to be. Unlike Plath, who in effect consciously prepared herself for a writing career from grade school on, Ann Lane focused much of her energy on learning domestic skills. As a child, she became an expert cook because she liked to eat and an expert seamstress at least in part because she was overweight and wanted to make her own clothes. She sold pound cakes in the neighborhood and did the family laundry, too. Like her parents, she was practical and relished doing all things well. In that sense, she was growing up in the classic New England tradition: a study in efficiency, thrift, and utility.

And, though her most famous character, Lutie Johnson, would be deceived by Benjamin Franklin's optimistic guidelines for achievement, Ann Lane and her family were not deceived; they were convinced. "My parents truly believed that early to bed, early to rise would make *any person* healthy, wealthy, and wise," Petry writes. "They had two daughters, so they did not say this would make a *man* healthy, wealthy, and wise but that it would have this effect on *any person.* So we rose at 6:00 A.M., went to bed promptly at 10:00 P.M. as regularly as clockwork" (*CAAS,* 262). Thus, from an early age, Ann learned both the discipline espoused by a Founding Father and the way to apply that discipline to herself: change the shell of language, keep the kernel of truth. It was a lesson not always easy, or even possible, for many of her fellow blacks to apply—then or now.

Ann Lane grew up with books mostly by and about white people. She read nineteenth-century American authors, many of them associated with New England, including Hawthorne, Poe, Harriet Beecher Stowe, and Louisa May Alcott. Sybil Weir has argued that Petry's New England literary heritage comes through in her fiction, especially in the characterization of Abbie Crunch in *The Narrows:* "Abbie is almost an elderly version of Stowe's Topsy [in *Uncle Tom's Cabin*], who incorporated the white contempt for blacks into her own self-concept."[6] But Petry herself offers only this contradictory observation: "I don't think that New England had any particular influence on my writing. Though I was born in this area I was not a New Englander. I have been influenced by Thoreau. His account of his life on Walden Pond made me realize how superficial and unimportant most of the trappings were with which I had surrounded myself" (*CAAS,* 267). Clearly Petry, who has been *in* New England most of her long life, is also *of* it, even if her race has made her feel like an outsider at times. And even she admits, somewhat grudgingly, that her family was in some ways representative of the region: "We were all of us, in my family, influenced by that old New England dictum: use it up, wear it out, make it do, or do without. And I still am. In that sense, I suppose I am a New Englander though there must be other parts of the United States where being thrifty and frugal are regarded as virtues" (*CAAS,* 267).

Pharmacist Turned Professional Writer

Two years after graduating from high school, she enrolled in the Connecticut College of Pharmacy, now part of the University of Connecticut. In New Haven she studied the sciences and prepared herself for a career in the family business. After graduation, she worked for several years in the Old Saybrook shop and the other drugstore the Lanes had acquired in Old Lyme. She and her sister would sometimes visit with relatives in Hartford, and it was there that she met her future husband, George Petry of New Iberia, Louisiana. The couple married 28 February 1938 in the Lane home.

The marriage was a turning point for Ann Lane Petry, then twenty-nine. With her husband she moved to New York, leaving behind her career as a pharmacist as well as the tranquility of her hometown. In New York, George managed a restaurant while Ann turned her attention to journalism, specifically two weekly Harlem newspapers. After three years of selling ad space for the *Amsterdam News,* she took a job with the *People's Voice,* where she edited the women's pages and worked as a general news reporter from 1941 to 1944.

Traversing the littered streets of Harlem, living for the first time among large numbers of poor black people, seeing neglected children up close—Petry's early years in New York inevitably made painful impressions on her. In addition to doing newspaper work, she also helped run an after-school program at a Harlem grade school. As she recollects the experience, "I worked at P.S. 10 on St. Nicholas and 116th Street in an after-school program for door-key kids. . . . Although I had been aware of Harlem, this was [my] first realization of the impact of that kind of hard life on kids. I lived my whole life without paying attention. It wasn't my life. But once I became aware, I couldn't see anything but" (Fein, B2). Reading to the children and teaching them arts and crafts was a way of making their lives a little better, but Petry could not ignore the realities waiting for her young charges once they went home. One little boy told her "he lived with a lady—he didn't even know what her name was. . . . This to me came as a shock, an absolute shock. Even though I had been living near Harlem, I don't think you're ever aware of children or what happens to them unless you've been put in a situation like that" (Streitfeld, E2).

Ann Lane Petry had not known until moving to New York the extent of adversity many blacks faced. Cloistered in the bosom of her family in Old Saybrook, commended by teachers, oblivious to the impoverishment of urban blacks, she had lived her first three decades in a kind of bubble where racism and sexism did not often intrude. She had grown up hearing tales of family members who had endured degradation—the maternal grandfather who ran away from slavery in Virginia, the great-uncle arrested for being in a Georgia town after sundown, and even her father, who was threatened by a white man when he opened the drugstore—but the family legacy was all about survival and success rather than defeat and despair. Even her encounter with racism at age four was quickly quelled and reframed as a victory.

So it was with mixed feelings of hope and horror that Petry entered into the strange, fascinating world of Harlem. The Harlem Renaissance of the 1920s was over; the black writers associated with that era, including Langston Hughes, Jean Toomer, Nella Larsen, and Zora Neale Hurston, were no longer in the public eye. The stock market crash of 1929, the Depression, and the onset of World War II were national, all-consuming preoccupations, and many of the white patrons who had helped bankroll the Harlem Renaissance were no longer able to support it or perhaps just no longer interested in their old cause. Young black women, who had little opportunity for formal education beyond high school, routinely accepted domestic work because that was the line of employment open to them:

> On the eve of the war, according to the 1940 census, 59.5 percent of employed Black women were domestic workers and another 10.4 percent worked in non-domestic service occupations. Since approximately 16 percent still worked in the fields, scarcely one out of ten Black women workers had really begun to escape the old grip of slavery. Even those who managed to enter industry and professional work had little to boast about, for they were consigned, as a rule, to the worst-paid jobs in these occupations.[7]

The onset of World War II provided thousands of black women with jobs in industry, but that did not eliminate the fact that many others remained in domestic labor and would continue to do so after the war. And the circumstances for domestics were often deeply humiliating: "Even in the 1940s, there were street-corner markets in New York and other large cities—modern versions of slavery's auction block—inviting white women to take their pick from the crowds of Black women seeking work" (Davis, 95). Add to this the crime and violence Petry saw and recorded as a reporter, and the picture of her new life in and around Harlem appears to be an exceptionally bleak one.

But instead of destroying her confidence, her new environment galvanized her imagination and precipitated the publications that brought her into the spotlight. She looked at Harlem with the dual vision of an outsider, who had not grown up with the problems endemic to ghetto life, and an insider, who identified with the people of her own race and wanted to put their struggle into words. Her breakthrough as a fiction writer occurred in December 1943 when the *Crisis* (published by the National Association for the Advancement of Colored People) published "On Saturday the Siren Sounds at Noon." It was not her first published story—that had been "Marie of the Cabin Club" printed in 1939 by the *Afro-American,* a Baltimore weekly[8]—but it was the story that caused a Houghton Mifflin editor to write to Petry and ask if she were working on a novel. The publishing company offered literary fellowships for promising manuscripts, and the editor hoped Petry would consider applying for the fellowship.

The work that caught the editor's eye was a two-page story describing a black child's death by fire, the murder of the child's mother, and the subsequent suicide of her murderer and husband. If she had written it as a straightforward narrative in chronological order, the story would probably have sunk under the weight of its own doom. But Petry opted for a more subtle approach, setting the story mostly in the mind of the unnamed man whose wife, Lilly Belle, had locked their children inside the day a fire swept through the apartment. As the man stands on a subway platform, he is overwhelmed by the wail of an air-raid siren. The horrific noise causes him to relive the events of the previous Monday, when he came home to discover the fire's ravages: his youngest child dead, the others lying bandaged in Harlem Hospital. Lilly Belle, dressed in mourning clothes, had tried to explain away her absence. That Saturday morning, though, he had overheard a neighbor spilling the truth:

> Cora was talking. "You ain't never been no damn good. And if you don't quit runnin' to that bar with that dressed up monkey and stayin' away from here all day long, I'm goin' to tell that poor fool you're married to where you were when your kid burned up in here." She said it fast as though she wanted to get it out before Lilly Belle could stop her. "You walkin' around in mournin' and everybody but him knows you locked them kids in here that day. They was locked in—"[9]

The revelation brings the man to his feet and causes him to strangle his wife. The story then flashes forward to the present, when the man's train finally arrives: "Just as it reached the edge of the platform, he jumped. The wheels ground his body into the gleaming silver of the tracks" ("On Saturday," 369). While the plot, packed into so brief a space, teeters dangerously close to melodrama, the eerie calm of the narration and its framing in the tortured man's mind make this a memorable story.

In addition to heralding the beginning of Petry's career, "On Saturday the Siren Sounds at Noon" has a special significance because it contains key elements familiar to readers of her later work. Betrayal, deep-seated anger, and murderous violence all recur in her three novels. Understated, exact description and the use of indirect discourse to convey a character's thoughts are also hallmarks of Petry's fiction. The screeching siren, furthermore, shows Petry applying the premises of naturalism: the terrible noise that the man hears is equalled and exceeded by the noise in his own anguished mind. His environment not only reflects his torment but contributes to it. The invisible walls of oppression locking his family into tenement life are manifested in the locked door preventing his children's escape. And Lilly Belle, though an unsympathetic character on the surface, is pathetic deep down. Her husband threatens to kill her if she leaves the children at home alone; she responds that she just wants to have "some fun" in her life ("On Saturday," 368). Fun is not on the horizon for anyone in this story, and the options available to these characters—the dreary routine of poverty or the shock of sudden death—are in fact foregone conclusions.

The Big Break

Petry's life was not nearly so hopeless. Though her husband was drafted and the *People's Voice* went out of business, she decided, with the Houghton Mifflin editor's encouragement in mind, that the time had come for her to write a novel. She took a part-time typing job and completed a freelance project writing copy for a wig manufacturer. This income, plus allotment checks from George, provided the resources she needed to begin the manuscript that would become *The Street*. She knew that writing on a schedule, as well as living frugally, would be essential: "I began my first novel, writing every day from 9:00 a.m. to noon, and then stopping for an hour for lunch and writing from 1:00 p.m. to 2:30 or 3:00 p.m. Every day" (*CAAS*, 265). The discipline paid off in 1945 when Houghton Mifflin awarded her a $2,400 fellowship for her work in progress. She had submitted five chapters, a synopsis, and two letters of recommendation. Fueled by the fellowship, she completed the novel in time for publication the following year. Writing it allowed her to build on the themes glimpsed in "On Saturday the Siren Sounds at Noon" and to develop her eye for detail and character. The first chapter, in which Lutie Johnson makes her way along the dirty, windy street to the tenement that will become her new home, came to Petry in a burst of creativity. But the rest came more slowly:

> That first chapter is about as good as a first chapter can be. I went over the book, not that chapter, but the rest of it, over and over and over again, simplifying it, testing the dialogue, the descriptions of people and places. I put all of my feelings, my sense of outrage into the book. I tried to include the sounds and the smells and the sights of Harlem. I wanted a book that was like an explosion inside the head of the reader, a book that you couldn't put down once you'd started reading it. I tried to create a vivid sense of place. (*CAAS*, 265)

Petry's comments are reminiscent of Richard Wright's aims in writing *Native Son*, which preceded *The Street* by six years. In "How 'Bigger' Was Born," Wright explains that he felt terrible misgivings after publishing his collection of short stories, *Uncle Tom's Children:* "When the reviews of that book began to appear, I realized that I had made an awfully naive mistake. I found that I had written a book which even bankers' daughters could read and weep over and feel good about. I swore to myself that if I ever wrote another book, no one would weep over it; that it would be so hard and deep that they would have to face it without the consolation of tears."[10]

Both Wright and Petry were intent on creating gritty, realistic works that would grip their readers and awaken them to social problems they probably knew little of first-hand. Both succeeded. Wright's portrait of Bigger Thomas, a poor black Chicago youth tried for the murder of Mary Dalton, a young white woman, was the benchmark achievement in black American fiction before 1950 and a seminal work in the protest tradition. His use of naturalistic detail—the repeated contrasts between the darkness and filth of Bigger's impoverished life with the lightness and cleanliness of the wealthy Daltons' life of privilege—evoked the methods of Theodore Dreiser and Stephen Crane, but in its relentless focus on American racism it was fresh, bold, even shocking.

In the character of Bigger Thomas, Wright created an effective vehicle for both the causes and effects of racism. Desperately poor, uneducated, and unable to love or respect himself, Bigger turns to violence as a means of escaping the hopeless mire of his existence. Both his unintentional killing of Mary Dalton and his ruthless murder of his girlfriend Bessie Mears result from his fears of whites and the control they exert over him. His attempt to ransom Mary Dalton after her death is as pathetic as it is devious: It is his one chance to gain power over the race that has made his life a tunnel of resentment and despair. But no one in this book ever really has the upper hand. The white people's reaction to Bigger the murderer, the mass clamor for his execution, suggests the bottomless depths of their own fears. A power struggle requires two sides, and the white power brokers in *Native Son* are just as frightened, just as capable of irrational behavior, as Bigger himself.

Likewise, in *The Street,* Petry portrays both the causes and effects of racism in midcentury America. But in contrast with *Native Son, The Street* focuses on a black woman with some education and ambition rather than a black man with little of either. Lutie's prospects are ultimately not much different from Bigger's; neither can penetrate the real and invisible barriers holding them back and down. But Lutie, an attractive young woman, faces a problem that Bigger knows about only as a perpetrator. The vicious sexism Lutie confronts at every turn is as much her conqueror as racism is. Petry's convincing portrayal of the plight of a black woman thus takes Wright's vision a step further, since racism and sexism inevitably and unfortunately go hand in hand.

A Representative Woman

The Street had something else in common with *Native Son* besides a naturalistic style and a focus on racism: It made the author famous. The book attracted both critical and popular attention and quickly sold more than 1.5 million copies in hardcover and paperback. Suddenly Ann Petry was a sought-after novelist, not an anonymous young woman typing away while her husband was off at war. Her success was quickly embraced by magazines published for a black audience. In a feature called "Ann Petry Planned to Write," *Opportunity* exclaimed that *"The Street,* a mere milestone for Ann Petry, is highly gratifying as an achievement, because it is the result of a *planned career."*[11] The *Crisis,* reminding readers that "On Saturday the Siren Sounds at Noon" appeared in its pages, celebrated Petry's success as the magazine's own: "Mrs. Petry thus joins that company of brilliant young writers, Langston Hughes, et al., who first received publication in the pages of the *Crisis."*[12] And *Ebony's* feature on

Petry's publication party hinted that the author's impressive debut, like
Wright's, meant progress for the whole race:

> Ann Petry was launched, much in the same fashion as a new ship except
> for the champagne bottle, at a cocktail party held in New York's Hotel
> Biltmore by her publishers, Houghton-Mifflin. Her debut was attended
> by over 200 guests who downed large quantities of liquor, consumed
> several huge trays of hors d'oeuvres and indulged in a surplus of conver-
> sation. By and large the evening was a success—many guests left con-
> vinced that they had participated in a significant event in American
> literary history.
>
> Of those invited to the cocktail party 40 per cent were Negroes.
> Although the novel went on sale the following day, after having rolled up
> an advance sale of 20,000, most of the guests had already read it. From
> the moment the first guests started arriving at 5:30 P.M. to the departure
> of the last some two hours later, Ann Petry's brilliant first novel was vig-
> orously discussed.[13]

Ann Petry thus became a representative figure, a black woman whose
achievement was recognized by a white publishing company and white
readers. Her stature was at least as important to the black community as
the difficult subject matter of *The Street.*

By and large the reviews of Petry's first novel were extremely favor-
able. Notices in the white press applauded the book. The *Crisis* editor
who had praised Petry in a feature story, however, had nothing good to
say about *The Street.* James W. Ivy seems horrified that Petry refused to
gloss over the ugly side of Harlem:

> There is much explicit factuality in the book, and no doubt the author
> can cite chapter and verse for every episode she sets down, yet the total
> picture is a distortion. Harlem is not the seething cesspool of sluts, pimps,
> juvenile delinquents, and clucks pictured in this novel. There are normal
> and responsible people in the community but you would never suspect it
> from reading this book. The jacket describes the book as "a living portrait
> of Harlem." But it is worthless as a picture of Harlem though interesting
> as a revelation of Mrs. Petry.[14]

Ivy's defensive reaction to the book suggests that he was appalled that a
woman with "a creamy-brown complexion; alert, smiling eyes; and a soft
cultivated voice" could write such a forceful, ultimately violent book
(Ivy, 48). Perhaps he wanted *The Street* to be as pleasant a work as Petry
was a person. Roger William Riis, the reviewer for *Opportunity,* took a

much different view. Although he thought the book lacked control and was heavy-handed at times—"the worst flaw is the wholesale way in which she lays on tragedy when she wants tragedy"—he applauded the overall effect of *The Street:* "Mrs. Petry has painted impressively the desolate sense of being blocked and barred off, of 'looking through a hole in a wall at some enchanted garden,' and being forever unable to pass the wall. It is a barrier which shuts out millions of Americans, and it is a barrier which has no rightful place among human beings of any nation, perhaps least of all ours."[15]

After publishing *The Street,* Petry was besieged with letters, phone calls, and demands on her time that she had neither expected nor wanted. When her husband returned from the service, he found that he was married to a celebrity. Also a writer, specializing in detective fiction, he was definitely in a supporting role as soon as *The Street* hit the bookstands. *Ebony* reported that "he admitted having a mild resentment at being introduced as 'Ann Petry's husband'" ("First Novel," 36). Ann Petry, meanwhile, after nearly a decade of city life that wound up with a spotlight turned her way, wanted to go home.

Return to Old Saybrook

The couple found a large eighteenth-century house in Old Saybrook; it was to be their permanent residence. They settled back into the small New England town that Ann Petry had known her whole life. Her next two novels, *Country Place* and *The Narrows,* would be about northern towns similar to her home turf, and her focus would expand to include many more white characters, perhaps a reflection of her environment as well as her interest in experimenting with content and style. Although she was now a public figure, whom many people would want to meet, Petry was determined to fashion a life of privacy for herself.

From her debut in 1946 through the publication of *Miss Muriel* in 1971, reviewers from publications both national and provincial have praised Petry's clear writing style and her ability to bring characters to life. Her sheer talent as a storyteller seems to conquer, at least temporarily, whatever racial or gender prejudices her readers might have.

In time, she would also make a name for herself as a writer of children's books. *The Drugstore Cat* (1949, illustrated by Susanne Suba) concerns Buzzy, a kitten taken in by the James family (James was Petry's mother's maiden name). An impetuous kitten, Buzzy soon realizes that while he can't communicate with everybody in the neighborhood, he can

"talk" to old people and children. At first he does not understand why
this is, but finally, after several adventures, he concludes that "Very, very
young people and very, very old people understand everything better
than anyone else. That's why Peter and Mr. Smith can understand cat
language."[16]

Petry's other book for children, *Legends of the Saints* (1970, illustrated
by Anne Rockwell), recounts the lives of saints in clear, descriptive language. The sketches subtly advocate the value of living a life of courage,
honesty, and humility.

Petry's two books for teenaged readers, *Harriet Tubman: Conductor on
the Underground Railroad* (1955) and *Tituba of Salem Village* (1964), reflect
her commitment to educating young people about African-American
history. In her autobiographical essay she explains, "When I write for
children I write about survivors: Tituba of Salem Village, indicted for
witchcraft in the seventeenth century; Harriet Tubman who helped run-
away slaves escape from the South before the Civil War" (*CAAS,* 253).
In *Harriet Tubman,* Petry intersperses narrative chapters with short, itali-
cized summaries of American history paralleling Tubman's life. The book
places Tubman at the center of a history that until very recently placed
black slave women firmly on the margins: "In many ways she represented the end of an era, the most dramatic, and the most tragic, era in
American history. Despite her work as a nurse, a scout, and a spy, in the
Civil War, she will be remembered as a conductor on the Underground
Railroad, the railroad to freedom—a short, indomitable woman, sustained by faith in a living God, inspired by the belief that freedom was a
right all men should enjoy, leading bands of trembling fugitives out of
Tidewater Maryland" (*CAAS,* 241). In this biography that reads like a
novel, Petry seeks to rectify the problem she identifies in the book's jacket copy: "It is my belief . . . that the majority of textbooks used in high
schools do not give an adequate or accurate picture of the history of slavery in the United States."[17]

Likewise, in *Tituba of Salem Village,* Petry tells a historical story in a
way that makes it accessible to readers of all races. The book gives
Tituba depth and humanity and shows how her would-be persecutors
willfully misunderstood the slave woman's creativity and kindness.

Without being overly didactic, both *Tituba of Salem Village* and
Harriet Tubman provide powerful black female role models for children
and teens while also filling in gaps in American history. In her 1969
essay "The Common Ground," Petry explains her goals as a writer for
young readers:

Over and over again, I have said: These are people. Look at them, listen to them; watch Harriet Tubman in the nineteenth century, a heroic woman, a rescuer of other slaves. Look at Tituba in the seventeenth century, a slave involved in the witchcraft trials in Salem Village. Look at them and remember them. Remember for what a long, long time black people have been in this country, have been a part of America: a sturdy, indestructible, wonderful part of America, woven into its heart and into its soul.[18]

The human, spiritual dimension is always central to Petry's writing, and she has made it clear that touching her young readers' hearts is as important to her as touching their minds. In "The Common Ground," she recounts a surprise encounter she had with a child returning *Harriet Tubman* to the Old Saybrook library. The anecdote functions as a metaphor for that all-important connection between children's authors and their readers:

I had never had a face-to-face encounter with a young reader who was actually holding one of my books. The child looked at me, and I looked at her—she didn't say anything and neither did I. I didn't know what to say. Neither did she. Finally she reached out and touched my arm, ever so gently, and then drew her hand back as though she were embarrassed. I copied her gesture, touching her gently on the arm, because I felt it would serve to indicate that I approved her gesture. ("Common Ground," 71)

The Petrys have a daughter, Elisabeth, now an attorney and author, to whom *Harriet Tubman* is dedicated. Elisabeth's birth was "probably the greatest gift that my husband and I have had bestowed upon us" (*CAAS,* 268), and the family apparently remains as close as the Lane family always was. Such familial compatibility contrasts sharply with the ways of the characters in Petry's novels. Their inability to trust each other, to form mutually satisfying bonds, often precipitates the crises in which they repeatedly find themselves. Her own life illustrates the values these characters either do not possess or cannot effectively bring to bear on their daily lives.

Petry's Renaissance

Though Ann Petry agreed to a round of interviews when Houghton Mifflin reissued *The Street* in 1992, she remains protective of her time and energy. Interviewers routinely describe her as much more friendly with them than their taped conversations with her would suggest. In interviews, Petry tends to answer questions as succinctly as possible, often providing her interlocutor with little basis for follow-up questions. Although Petry is not always taciturn, the following excerpt from a 1989 interview is characteristic of her interview style:

> Q. Upon writing and publishing your first short story, "Marie of the Cabin Club," you used the pen name Arnold Petri. Why a pseudonym? Was it because you were then a would-be writer? Or a woman? Or . . .
>
> A. Neither. I am a "private person." I did not want my friends, acquaintances, and colleagues to know that I was writing short stories.
>
> Q. The story has one of the most favorable portrayals of a black man: Georgie Barr is a gentleman, well-traveled, successful, articulate, handsome, heroic, and something of an 007-adventurous type. There isn't a blemish. I realize I have made a comment here, but will you comment?
>
> A. No comment is necessary.
>
> Q. Well, is there a conscious effort after this story to portray a less romantic and a more representational black male?
>
> A. No.[19]

Despite such daunting brevity, Petry is well-known among scholars of African-American literature for her willingness to correspond with them about her work. Seemingly determined to control her public image, she prefers the security of correspondence to the spontaneity of conversation.

Always read and always recognized by a dedicated cadre of critics, Petry has in the past decade begun to receive national honors for career achievement. She holds honorary doctorates from Suffolk University (1983), the University of Connecticut (1988), and Mount Holyoke College (1989). She was the subject of the "Ann Petry Conference," a literary conference bringing together literary critics and Connecticut high school teachers and students at Trinity College in Hartford in 1992. During that conference, she was honored with a mayoral proclamation declaring 14 November 1992 "Ann Petry Day." And she has received honorary citations from the City of Philadelphia (1985) and the United Nations Association (1988).

Petry has entered into the public arena in other ways as well. In addition to corresponding with scholars and teachers over the years, she has donated many of her manuscripts and private papers to university libraries, including the Mugar Memorial Library, Boston University; the African-American Research Center, Shaw University; the Beinecke Rare Book and Manuscript Library, Yale University; the Woodruff Library,

Atlanta University; and the Moorland-Spingarn Research Center, Howard University.

In 1986, Petry's story "The Moses Project" appeared in the *Harbor Review,* a literary journal published by the University of Massachusetts, Boston.[20] As her books find their way onto college syllabuses across the country, Petry's writing is attracting a new generation of readers and literary critics. Like the characters in her stories and novels, Petry's readers are diverse in age, race, and attitude. Yet they find a kinship within the realistically drawn worlds of Petry's fictional communities.

Chapter Two
Ann Petry's Troubled Communities

We remember some quintessentially American authors as much for the communities where their characters live as for the characters themselves. To think of Faulkner, for instance, is to think of Yoknapatawpha County, Mississippi. To think of Willa Cather is to think of Black Hawk, Nebraska. Sherwood Anderson is likewise linked with Winesburg, Ohio; Zora Neale Hurston with Eatonville, Florida; Thomas Wolfe with Altamont, North Carolina. While all of these writers are realists whose keen eye for physical detail adds considerably to their fiction's mood and meaning, we may rightly view their evocation of particular places as an important end in itself.

A community—real or fictional—simultaneously reflects and determines the individual members' identities. The size of the population, the racial and ethnic mix, the distribution of wealth and education, and the opportunities for employment are among the factors characterizing a town. These same factors may collectively dictate who succeeds and who fails, who marries and who stays single, who feels accepted and who feels rejected, who remains a lifetime and who leaves abruptly. Writing realistically about a community means writing about not just the whole, not just individual parts, but also the dynamic relationships between the whole community and its individual members. Such a portrayal is an extraordinarily complex undertaking.

Although Faulkner is the American author generally credited with accomplishing such an aim, the same may be said of Ann Petry. Petry's detailed portraits of communities are central to *The Street* (1946), *Country Place* (1947), *The Narrows* (1953), and *Miss Muriel and Other Stories* (1971).[1] Like Faulkner, Petry examines a wide range of individuals and their relationships with each other, and she takes pains to place her examination of race relations in the context of an American community. But while Faulkner returns repeatedly to the intricacies of life in Yoknapatawpha County, Petry moves back and forth between urban, fragmented communities and small, insular ones. Her focus on relationships within the community, moreover, anticipates the work of younger African-American women authors such as Toni Morrison, Gloria Naylor, and Alice Walker.

As a native of Old Saybrook, Connecticut, a picturesque resort community on the Connecticut River, Petry is intimately acquainted with small-town New England. Except for her nine years in New York City after her marriage to George Petry in 1938 and a year teaching at the University of Hawaii in the mid-1970s, Petry has lived in Old Saybrook for her entire life. In her fictional portrayals of small towns in Connecticut and New York, she draws on her family background as the daughter of the town pharmacist, her firsthand knowledge of the region's terrain and climate, and her observations of the way people in small towns interact. She goes far beyond her own viewpoint as a native daughter of Old Saybrook, however, by exploring northern communities from various perspectives of race, gender, social class, and age, and by refusing to flinch from graphic depictions of racial prejudice and violence. The overall result is a multifaceted portrait of small-town New England, where the pretty surface barely conceals a morass of social prejudices—some racial, others related to gender, sexual orientation, and age.

Since Petry lived in Harlem during the 1940s and worked there for several years as a journalist, it is not surprising that her descriptions of wartime Harlem are just as detailed and realistic as her descriptions of little New England towns. Her portrayal of the urban North is generally a bleak one. In contrast to her fictional small towns, there is no pretense of a pretty surface in Petry's vision of Harlem. For most of her black characters there, life boils down to the horrors of racial subjugation. In her most sustained portraits of Harlem—such as *The Street* and "In Darkness and Confusion"—the ghetto is a sad, painful place to live. The urban black characters' suffering is especially acute once they come to believe that there is no better life ahead, that the American dream of success is not theirs to strive for, let alone achieve.

By surveying the communities that are prominent in Petry's three novels and her collection of short fiction, we can see how integral communities are to her work.[2] In her novels and stories, Petry goes to great lengths to show how people respond to their physical and social environments. While this may suggest a heavy debt to naturalism and social determinism (and hence to precursors such as Stephen Crane, Theodore Dreiser, and Richard Wright), Petry goes beyond the narrative strictures of these two ultimately formulaic philosophies.[3] Far from simplistic puppets of nature, her characters are emotionally complex, stubborn, and willful. The complicated tensions between these characters and their

communities are at the heart of Petry's fictional enterprise. The following overview of Petry's major fictional communities will provide a context for discussions of the personal relationships central to *The Street,
Country Place, The Narrows,* and *Miss Muriel.*

"Shameful and unjustifiable": Ann Petry's Harlem

Petry became intimately acquainted with Harlem during her decade
there, from 1938 to 1947. Since her husband had been drafted into the
Army, she experienced the city mostly as an independent working
woman. At various times during the 1940s, she was a teacher, copy-
writer, newspaper journalist, consumer advocate, actress, and student at
Columbia University.[4] In retrospect, this immersion in Harlem culture
seems to have been just the education Petry needed to write *The Street,*
her first novel.

Petry's essay on Harlem in the April 1949 issue of *Holiday* offers a
useful point of departure for discussing her fictional portrayal of Harlem.
This long essay (published after she and her husband had returned to
Old Saybrook) is a kind of manifesto detailing Petry's social convictions
as well as her observations of the city. She catalogues neighborhoods
(Sugar Hill, the Hollow, Spanish Harlem); streets (125th Street, Seventh
Avenue, Lenox Avenue); landmarks (the City Market, the Hotel Theresa,
Sydenham Hospital); clubs (the Apollo, Small's Paradise); famous
Harlemites (W. E. B. Du Bois, Walter White); and frequent visitors
(Lena Horne, Joe Louis). Through imagery and anecdote, she supports
her claim that Harlem is "as varied and as full of ambivalences as
Manhattan itself."[5] The following passage exemplifies the essay's zesty
flavor:

> [Harlem] is a hodgepodge of churches, bars, beauty parlors, harsh
> orange-red neon signs, poolrooms, candy stores. It is a perspiring soapbox
> orator shouting from the top of a stepladder at the corner of Seventh
> Avenue and 125th Street, on a warm night in June; a hot roasted yam
> purchased from a pushcart and eaten on the street on a cold windy night;
> and the cricket matches at Van Cortlandt Park. It is the exclusive Comus
> Club giving a formal dance at the Savoy Ballroom; a woman crying,
> "Murder!" at three in the morning; a thick slice of ice-cold watermelon,
> honeysweet, bought on Lenox Avenue on a hot summer day; the barbe-
> cued ribs browning on a spit in the window of a Seventh Avenue restau-
> rant. And it is a real gone gal on stage at the Apollo Theater, so gone
> that the audience stamps and whistles, beating out the rhythm until the

Apollo's old walls tremble. It is a furtive man dropping numbers slips into the eager hands of a syndicate; and a calypso singer, at a Trinidadian carnival, in the spring of the year, half-talking, half-singing, "Always marry a woman uglier than you." ("Harlem," 164)

This paean to Harlem appeals to all sensory perceptions and embraces all kinds of activities—singing, dancing, drinking, eating, speechifying, gambling, exercising, and whistling. But murdering, gambling, and sexual one-upmanship (implicit in the Trinidadian chant) also find their way into Petry's panoramic tour of the community. No matter that she is writing for a travel magazine—she refuses to gloss over either Harlem's intimidating sensuality or its dangerously rough edges.

Bad housing is one especially rough-edged issue that Petry returns to again and again. In her essay, she laments "the ugly tenements and the scarred, evil-smelling rooms in the Hollow" ("Harlem," 116). Such degrading conditions ultimately overshadow the fruits of the community's fertile imagination: "And so Harlem is also two hundred persons jammed into seventy dingy, vermin-ridden rooms, in old-fashioned brownstones without fire escapes, on Lenox Avenue, and 123rd Street, their halls lightless, their stairs, corridors and lavatories filthy" ("Harlem," 116, 163). The somber conclusion argues that when Harlem is "looked at head on, its thousand faces finally merge into one—the face of a ghetto. In point of time it belongs back in the Middle Ages. Harlem is an anachronism—shameful and unjustifiable, set down in the heart of the biggest, richest city in the world" ("Harlem," 168). Petry's final words contrast dramatically with her enthusiasm for Harlem's vigorous social life. The allusion to the Middle Ages suggests that for all of its sensual charm, Harlem is moving backward toward obscurity and increasingly primitive living conditions: In the aftermath of the much-acclaimed Harlem Renaissance, the ghetto is an anonymous, primitive place where the sporadic bursts of laughter—and spontaneous flights of imagination—are the more dramatic for being so rare.

As a cultural anachronism, a place that cries out for clear-eyed representation, Harlem is ripe ground for a fiction writer of Petry's particular brand of realism. In her fiction as in her essay on Harlem, she juxtaposes the community's foot-stamping vitality with its dark-roomed destitution. But while her works set in Harlem generally take some notice of the pleasures that Harlem residents enjoy, they are primarily chronicles of poverty and oppression.

The two-page apprentice story that essentially launched her career, "On Saturday the Siren Sounds at Noon," captures the inescapable sense of oppression felt by the protagonist as an air-raid alarm precipitates his grim recollections: "It was everywhere around him, plucking at him, pounding at his ears. It was inside of him. It was his heart and it was beating faster and harder and faster and harder. He bent forwards because it was making a pounding pressure against his chest. It was hitting him in the stomach" ("On Saturday," 368). Once he has mentally retraced the awful events leading up to the murder of his wife and leaped to his death under a rushing train, "The air was filled with noise—the sound of the train and the wobble of the siren as it died away to a low moan. Even after the train stopped, there was a thin echo of the siren in the air" ("On Saturday," 369). The story ends on this eerily remorseless note.

"On Saturday the Siren Sounds at Noon" presents Petry's Harlem in its worst light. It is a community where despair reigns supreme, where the residents can find little solace even in their own homes. Their psychological hardships are mirrored in their unwelcoming surroundings, and it seems inevitable that in such a place family members would turn against one another. In this case, the claustrophobic environment not only contributes to the family's torment; it also underscores the anguish they experience in a racist society. Significantly, though, the protagonist and his wife are believable, rounded characters. Even as they embody a whole underclass, they linger in our minds just as the siren's noise echoes in the air. Such evocative characterization has consistently raised Petry's work to the level of art.

"On Saturday the Siren Sounds at Noon" paved the way for *The Street,* into which Petry poured a great deal of what she had observed, experienced, and felt in Harlem. "I put all of my feelings, my sense of outrage into the book," she writes in an autobiographical essay. "I tried to include the sounds and the smells and the sights of Harlem. . . . I tried to create a vivid sense of place" (*CAAS,* 265). Like her later essay on Harlem, her first novel would portray the urban black community from many different perspectives.

Probably because she had grown up in a community so different from Harlem, Petry was acutely aware of New York City's black section *as* a place—a place that, despite her racial kinship, she saw through the eyes of an outsider, a sheltered, small-town New Englander. This place alternately delighted, shocked, and saddened her. Finally, it moved her to immortalize the marginalized in her understated, distinctly unsentimental prose.

In *The Street,* Petry shows graphically how ghetto life can diminish even the hardiest souls, the most ambitious spirits. For every glimpse of cohesiveness, Petry includes a reminder of the community's unhappy subordination to the surrounding white society. A brief review of Lutie Johnson's few moments of optimism—and her subsequent feelings of despairing anger—will illustrate this pattern.

While Lutie rarely seeks out companionship, she is quick to observe other blacks enjoying each other's company. Early in the novel, for example, she notices that blacks emerging from the subway visibly relax once they are back in Harlem: "The same people who had made themselves small on the train, even on the platform, suddenly grew so large they could hardly get up the stairs to the street together." These adults are "talking and laughing" now that they are on their home turf.[6] Caught up in their high spirits, Lutie thinks that even 116th Street, where her tenement home awaits her, looks welcoming in the sunset's glow. She passes happily among children who are "playing ball and darting back and forth across the sidewalk in complicated games of tag" (64). Later, at the Casino, she witnesses another cheerful scene: "Some of the dancing couples jitter-bugged, did the rhumba, invented intricate new steps of their own. The ever-moving, ever-changing lights picked faces and figures out of the crowd; added a sense of excitement and strangely the quality of laughter to the dancers" (223). Singing at the Casino fills Lutie with a similar sense of belonging; she is thrilled when the men in the orchestra bow to her, "for she knew that this absurd, preposterous bowing was their way of telling her they were accepting her on merit as a singer, not because she was Boots' newest girl friend" (222). For once, Lutie is part of the crowd, even the star of the crowd, rather than the perennial victim of bad times and bad luck.

But pleasures in Harlem, even such vivid ones, quickly and inevitably give way to the torpor of ghetto life. While Lutie and her fellow Harlem residents may feel larger and more relaxed in their own community, they cannot let their guard down completely; they cannot altogether stop being "small" just because they are at home. In a butcher's shop manned by "a fat red-faced man with a filthy apron tied around his enormous stomach" (61), Lutie thinks with distaste of the Eighth Avenue store's sparse offerings and its unsanitary conditions. When she walks along Eighth Avenue on another occasion, she silently excoriates "the mean little stores" that sell "the leavings, the sweepings, the impossible unsalable merchandise, the dregs and dross that were reserved especially for Harlem" (153). In a community where almost everybody is black, white people retain control of the quality—and quantity—of basic necessities. The ghetto's commodities are just as bad as its living conditions.

As for the happily playing children, Lutie comes down the sunlit street to find her own son working as a shoeshine boy. At age eight, he is too worried about money to join the crowds of children playing on the street. His own pathetic games have to do with two mongrel dogs he watches from the apartment window. Looking through the window with her son, Lutie feels nothing of the optimism she had experienced walking home: "All through Harlem there were apartments just like this one, she thought, and they're nothing but traps. Dirty, dark, filthy traps. Upstairs. Downstairs. In my lady's chamber. Click goes the trap when you pay the first month's rent. Walk right in. It's a free country. Dark little hallways. Stinking toilets" (73). Her idealistic image of herself as a latter-day Ben Franklin, striving toward inevitable success, vanishes in the face of her oppressive circumstances. Long before she kills Boots Smith, she doubts that the American dream will be hers to realize.

Even Lutie's pleasures at the Casino are short-lived and illusory. On her first night at the club, she notices that the dancing throngs are not paying much attention to her, and Boots Smith's attentions have more to do with her looks than her voice. To her dismay, Lutie eventually discovers that Boots, like his boss Junto, sees her as a sexual pawn who does not deserve a salary, no matter how well she sings. The discovery abruptly ends her singing career. Lutie no longer sees the world through "a blur and a mist of happiness and contentment because she had found the means of getting away from the street" (223). For every blurred glimpse of hope in Harlem, there is also a wall of despair.

Such is the case for all of the novel's characters, not just Lutie. Other people in her apartment building—Bub, Mrs. Hedges, Jones, and Min—also suffer under the weight of racial oppression. Given the characters' miserable plights, Barbara Christian observes, "In *The Street* Harlem does not emerge as a community, for everyone is competing with everyone else for whatever each can get. Cut off from each other, the people merely pass one another, touching only when they must or when it is to their advantage."[7] Although Christian uses the term "community" in the connotative sense of mutual trust and affection and is therefore correct in her assertions, one may also argue that the disaffection and alienation of Petry's Harlem characters *create* the community— that is, give it a clearly defined identity. I argue in chapter 3 that Lutie's difficult relationships represent the terms of that identity: The 116th Street tenement-dwellers are unified by their degraded past and their bleak future. Most of them, moreover, are not about to leave town. Lutie's departure is the exception to the rule. The rest of her cohorts accept Harlem not just as their community but as their world—"shameful and unjustifiable" though it may be—a world they would not have chosen but which nevertheless seems to have chosen them.

As in *The Street,* the moments of humor and gentleness in the Harlem stories are poignant for being so rare. "Like a Winding Sheet" begins with a black couple preparing, companionably, for a long night at their factory jobs. They joke and chat with each other in a friendly manner. But after Johnson's racially charged encounter with his white female boss and several other incidents that raise his ire, his pent-up frustration is so fierce that he beats his wife for playfully calling him "nigger." As much as he has always prided himself on refusing to hit women, he is finally overwhelmed by rage: "He didn't let her finish what she was saying. She was standing close to him and that funny tingling started in his finger tips, went fast up his arms and sent his fist shooting straight for her face."[8] Though violence appears to be the only avenue of communication available to him, the assault on his wife will only exacerbate his troubles: It will ensure his alienation from the one person who provides him comfort and affection.

"In Darkness and Confusion," a detailed portrait of a Harlem race riot, begins on a note similar to "Like a Winding Sheet." William Jones is eating breakfast and listening to his wife, Pink, prepare for work. A comforting domesticity pervades the scene—we learn that he is having bacon, eggs, and cornbread for breakfast and that he can gauge Pink's progress by the sounds emanating from the bedroom—but Jones is too worried about his son, who is in the army, to enjoy his home life. It is not long before he is chastising himself for living in a Harlem tenement: "The rooms weren't big enough for a man to move around in without bumping into something. Sometimes he thought that was why Annie May spent so much time away from home. Even at thirteen she couldn't stand being cooped up like that in such a small amount of space" (261). Again, Petry emphasizes the dehumanizing effects of cramped housing, a theme running through many of her ghetto stories.

Like many of Petry's Harlem protagonists, Jones cannot sustain his hopes for a better life. Once he forfeits his dreams for his family, a terrible fury rushes into the void. When the riot erupts, he helps loot and ravage Harlem's stores. But the community's appearance of unified strength is only a guise for chaotic impotence. Pink's death and the arrest of Annie May, coupled with earlier news of his son Sam's court martial, are staggeringly heavy crosses for Jones to bear: As the mob gives way to police force, Jones is left all alone, shouting into the night. He never has a meaningful conversation with his family members; his one rebellion against authority takes from him the very people he most wanted to address. Thwarted communication is a prominent theme in Petry's short fiction, and Jones's situation is one of several in which the protagonist lashes out, violently and ineffectually, for lack of words to express the anguish of racism, the sadness of alienation from family, the pain of unacknowledged selfhood.

"The most beautiful street she had ever seen": *The Street*'s Lyme, Connecticut

Although *The Street* is primarily an urban novel, its narrative digression on Lyme provides a significant counterpoint to Lutie Johnson's life in Harlem. In contrast to the densely populated community of poor blacks in Harlem, Lyme is a secluded little pocket of prosperity on the Connecticut River. When Lutie Johnson takes a housekeeping job in Lyme with the Chandlers, a rich white family, she is awed by the town's natural grace. Filled with trees and sunlight, Lyme has "the most beautiful street she had ever seen" (29)—an ironic contrast to Harlem's 116th Street.[9] The Chandlers' home is also impressive. The antithesis of tenement living, it looks "so gracious with such long low lines, its white paint almost sparkling in the sun and the river very blue behind the house" (37). In short, Lyme is the diametric opposite of crowded, impoverished Harlem.

Her new employer's life, furthermore, contrasts sharply with Lutie's. Mrs. Chandler's clothes are new and expensive; Lutie's are old and cheap. Thanks to her successful husband, Mrs. Chandler works neither outside nor inside the home; with no support from her husband, Jim, Lutie works long hours as Mrs. Chandler's maid. Mrs. Chandler has ample time to socialize, while Lutie goes home to see her husband and son only once every two months (44). Finally, Mrs. Chandler can depend on her wealthy parents for support during times of crisis, but Lutie cannot depend on her alcoholic, unemployed father for anything except trouble.

Although Lutie feels that she has entered "a very strange world. . . . with an entirely different set of values" (41), she is not immune to the charms of life in Lyme. Her immersion in the Chandlers' materialistic culture causes her to come "more and more under the influence of their philosophy" (44). She begins to share their faith in the curative powers of wealth. Convinced that she and Jim "hadn't tried hard enough, worked long enough, saved enough" (43), she decides that the Chandlers' single-minded focus on money is the obvious means to a happy end.

Significantly, Lutie thinks of the Chandler household as one and the same with the community of Lyme. She comes to hate the town's beautiful main street (29), and she views the Chandlers' friends as a repugnant mass. The passing references to "Mr. Chandler and his friends" and "the young men who came up from New York to spend the weekend" suggest that Mr. Chandler, both an alcoholic and a workaholic, is a representative man of the worst kind (42). He personifies a whole class of privileged young white men whose shiny public images belie the tarnished truths of their private lives. Likewise, Mrs. Chandler's female friends appear insecure and shallow. Lutie notes that her employer "had a great many young friends who dressed just like she did—some of them even had small children about the age of Little Henry" (40). In Lutie's recollection, the women "ate like horses or they didn't eat at all, because they were afraid they would get too fat" (40). Within Lutie's earshot, they worry about exposing their husbands to attractive black maids. Like their husbands, these women are all show and no substance.

If the Chandlers are in fact typical of their community, as Petry's sweeping references to their friends would indicate, then Lyme as a whole is a depressing illusion: a pretty place where the residents lead uniformly bitter lives. Although the town is far more appealing on the surface than Harlem, the tangible trappings of the American dream mock, rather than assuage, their owners' feelings of inarticulate despair. In Lyme the "good life" is a two-faced god, frostily excluding marginalized outsiders like Lutie Johnson, while grimly confining miserable insiders like the Chandlers. Such a community is self-perpetuating as long as everyone is engaged in the same charade. The people of Lyme are united, ironically, in their preservation and deification of the "dream." A herd mentality accompanies their hubris. They will stick together, because they are not strong enough to strike out alone.

"To all appearances, a quiet, sleepy village": *Country Place*'s Lennox, Connecticut

Like Lyme, Lennox is a nearly all-white community that contrasts sharply with Petry's Harlem. But Lennox, the only community explored in *Country Place,* is a self-contained world, not a counterpoint to another

city or town. The characters in *Country Place,* furthermore, are not so
homogeneous—or monolithically shallow—as the wealthy residents of
Lyme. In the tradition of Sarah Orne Jewett, Sherwood Anderson, and
Edith Wharton, Petry scrutinizes the homely, sometimes poignant lives
of provincial whites. Unlike her predecessors, however, Petry is at least as
concerned with the evolving identity of the community as with individual characterization. In this respect, *Country Place* recalls, if only obliquely, Thoreau's philosophical depictions of places in *Walden* (1862) and
Cape Cod (1865).

One critic has argued that "the point of *Country Place* is that the town
is not happy. It is an aggregation of terrified individuals, anti-black, anti-
Semitic, anti-Catholic, and anti-themselves, who simultaneously seek
solace in each other and each others' annihilation."[10] But on closer
inspection *Country Place* seems much more concerned with the possibilities of perspective than with the limitations of unhappiness. Petry
explores the ways in which imagination and reality create each other
and, in doing so, both define and defy our notions of truth.

Lennox as a whole has a shifting identity. A tourist town in the summer, it suddenly becomes smaller and more insular every fall. The novel
begins in the fall, at that time of transformation. In the opening chapter,
the white pharmacist/narrator says that Lennox is "a quiet place, a country place, which sits at the mouth of the Connecticut River, at the exact
spot where the river empties itself into Long Island Sound."[11] There is a
town green, with George "Doc" Fraser's pharmacy on one side and the
Congregational Church on the other. Despite the fact that at summer's
end "Lennox becomes, to all appearances, a quiet, sleepy village," Doc
warns us at the outset that "truth has many sides" (4). He insists that
there is always more to a place than meets the eye.

The book contains the perspectives of eight characters in addition to
Doc, and each point of view adds to our composite knowledge of the
town and its residents. As first-person narrator, Doc claims to shape all
of the perspectives in the novel. Such assertions of omniscience render
him suspect, however, since his versions of people's private thoughts are
not necessarily the reliable reporting that he seems to think.
Furthermore, his protracted absences from the text suggest that another
narrator may well have wrested control away from him. In keeping with
these complications, Doc admits that his "true account" of the town
involves a great deal of imaginative speculation (4). In Lennox, as in
Thoreau's renderings of Walden and Cape Cod, reality is in the eye of
the beholder, and truth, in the hands of the narrator(s).

Doc's complex relationship with the storytelling "Weasel"—which I discuss in chapter 4—provides a key to the issues of narrative and authorial control at the crux of *Country Place*. Doc's absences from the story complicate matters even more. The frequent lapses into omniscient narration suggest the intrusion of another, unnamed narrator—one who seeks to illuminate relationships and situations that Doc could not know intimately. A concentric logic gradually emerges from *Country Place:* Every history is part of a larger fiction, and every author is a character in another author's story.

Throughout the book, Petry emphasizes the way that the reality of the whole town changes, depending on one's perspective and mood at the moment. During Johnnie Roane's short ride home from the train station, for instance, the young army veteran's opinion of Lennox shifts dramatically. One minute he is thrilled to be back in Lennox; the next he is remembering "all the things he had disliked about the town" (11). The taxi-driving Weasel's sly insinuations precipitate his disturbing thoughts. To Johnnie, the untrustworthy cabbie is "typical of the town's smugness, its satisfaction with itself, its sly poking fun at others" (11). Just listening to the Weasel reminds him that "the town wasn't big enough to hold him any more" (11). Johnnie quickly recognizes the disparity between the Lennox he sees and the Lennox he had imagined: "The town stinks, he thought. At least it's not what you remembered. And that isn't quite accurate. It is simply that you had forgotten the things you did not like about the town. You glossed them over and prettied them up and fondled them for four long years, until what you finally held was not this town" (12).

But illusions die hard. Johnnie is still thrilled by the smell of burning leaves and the sight of familiar old houses. The pleasures of the town that remain for him, however, are colored by his renewed feelings of ambivalence. His encounter with the Weasel has rekindled old dissatisfactions and sparked new doubts in his mind about Glory, his wife. Although he is home safely from the war, he is still on dangerous ground: For Johnny, the Weasel is an emblem of the hometown folks' prurient willingness to believe the worst about their neighbors and friends.

Johnnie's disillusionment with the town anticipates, and perhaps accelerates, his disillusionment with Glory. His encounter with the Weasel has put him on his guard. In his conversations with his wife, it becomes obvious that Glory's good looks are her most commendable feature. Like the town of Lennox, she is less appealing in person than in memory. There is both more and less to her than Johnnie would like there to be—more passion for living a life of her own, less interest in living with him.

Though immature, petulant, and ready to cheat on her husband, Glory is also genuinely oppressed by her marriage. She cannot envision herself as a mother, and her memories of her first year with Johnnie are far from happy. During her husband's four-year absence, she has found a niche for herself as a grocery-store clerk. She has also found, in Ed Barrell, the kind of low-class man that truly interests her. Her husband's return is thus an unwelcome intrusion. His insistence on storybook happiness with a beautiful wife clashes dreadfully with her preference for tabloid romance with the town stud.

Johnnie is too preoccupied with his own illusions to think about Glory's. The onset of a terrible storm accommodates his increasing anguish. As he approaches the cabin where he knows he will find his wife with Ed Barrell, the storm mirrors his rage at Glory and seems to validate his loathing for the whole town. His wife and Lennox are so inextricably linked in his mind that he cannot renounce one without wishing apocalypse on the other: "Once across the bridge he found he was enjoying the storm. I hope to Christ it wipes out the town of Lennox, leaving not a single building standing on its foundation, no blade of grass, no tree or shrub to mark the spot. I hope it destroys every plant; so that no one will ever know that people lived there. I want everyone to lose tonight" (186).

Johnnie's violent thoughts reveal both the powerful hold that the town has on him and the extent of his self-absorption. If he cannot be happy in Lennox, according to his logic, then the town no longer deserves to exist. But his death sentence for the town is also a death wish: If Lennox goes, he will go with it. Denied individual happiness, he clamors for communal tragedy: "I want all of them to be in at the death of their dreams; held there, immovable and defenseless, as they witness the last gasp" (186). This is hardly the homecoming Johnnie had imagined on first arrival; in the space of a few days, his attitude toward the town has swung from nostalgic affection to self-acknowledged ambivalence to unadulterated hatred. The town of his dreams has become the stuff of waking nightmares.

Johnnie's shifting views of Lennox are not the only indication that the reality of the town depends as much on people's perceptions as on their actions. His discussion of the town with his parents (before his rampage) provides further evidence of this. Johnnie's observation that the town "really doesn't change" sets off a dispute between his usually mild-mannered parents (125). His mother argues that the town has changed significantly over the years, while his father maintains that it has changed only in looks, not in substance. The main point of contention between husband and wife is the absence of "the fancy ladies and their gentlemen" who no longer vacation in the town (125). Mrs. Roane argues, perversely, that the presence of prostitutes had a positive influence on the girls of Lennox. The long-ago murder of one "fancy lady" was typical of the grim fates awaiting their kind, Mrs. Roane declares, concluding that the local girls benefited from these object lessons in morality: "They could see for themselves what could and did happen. Nowadays it's not so easy for a girl to see that. I blame the movies more than anything else. They make it easy for a girl to believe that somewhere there's a beautiful carefree life if they could just find it. Lots of them start looking for it without stopping to figure out how much it costs" (126).

Mrs. Roane thus makes a pointed reference to Glory's infatuation with movies—and with Ed Barrell. While her speech sounds pat, it raises several important issues about the role of illusion in determining the town's identity. The "fancy ladies" are themselves a fusion of illusion and reality. Their vacations with "the New York sports" are really assignations (125); their love lives, all business. Mr. Roane's recollection of the fascination that the women held for the town indicates, contrary to his wife's wishful thinking, that Lennox did not shun the women or censure their way of life. On the contrary, the locals eagerly attended the trial after the prostitute's murder. According to Mr. Roane, "'Quite a number of the fancy ladies had to testify and everybody wanted to get a good look at 'em'" (126). The crowds attending the trial no doubt experienced the same voyeuristic pleasures as Mrs. Roane's helplessly misguided moviegoers.

Since Mr. Roane and Mrs. Roane provide contradictory evidence, it is hard to say whether Lennox has changed for better or worse in recent years. It is clear, however, that the town is one thing in Mr. Roane's mind, another in Mrs. Roane's, yet another in Johnnie's. Like the movies and the fancy ladies, the town is subject and object rolled into one. While the community scrutinizes individual behavior, it is also the object of scrutiny. As such, it must bear the weight of a great many illusions and reproaches. The town becomes what its residents think it is. Its "reality" depends on their perspectives, memories, and imaginations.

The storm that builds and finally explodes in the novel is itself an imaginative device, driving all the characters toward self-revelation. Doc observes at the beginning, "I think that most of these things would have happened anyway, but because of the storm they took place sooner than they normally would have" (4). Regardless of that statement's accuracy, the storm provides Doc with a convenient conceit for his dramatic tale. Even its aftermath accommodates the novel's concern with shifting perceptions and slippery realities. Doc notes, "It might have been the morning of the first day—the day of Creation—a morning designed for a world that had not yet known pain and sorrow" (202). The uprooted trees and debris on the ground are evidence that the storm was real. But in retrospect, the storm seems much like the town—a swirl of truth and illusion, creation and re-creation: "As I looked at the sun shining on the church across the way," says Doc, "I remembered the awful tolling of the bells; remembered, too, the hideous howling of the wind—a wind so strong it had moved those massive bells back and forth as though they were made of straw" (203).

For Doc, the storm is now "a nightmare memory" (203), a haunting reminder of the chaos lurking around the edges of even the most peaceful scene. But by using the storm as a narrative device in his chronicle of Lennox, Doc is able to harness its chaotic force. As narrator (or at least one of the novel's narrators), Doc functions as a kind of god, controlling the timing and the impact of rain and wind. In this way, the "country place" he inhabits becomes the *Country Place* of his imagining.

Doc's imagined *Country Place* in turn merges with Petry's novel. The title of the novel reinforces her emphasis on the illusory, or fictional, qualities of reality. As readers, we inhabit *Country Place* just as Doc and his fellow citizens inhabit Lennox. We are inside a work of fiction just as they are inside the town. By reading and interpreting the book, furthermore, we create the town of Lennox in our minds just as its fictional citizens create it in theirs. Creating reality thus becomes the ultimate communal activity, joining people across time and boundary, both within and outside any designated place. As I argue in chapter 4, Doc's relationship with the Weasel helps us see the concentric circles of reality and illusion involved in any narrative. For in this novel, it is impossible to say where Doc's notion of a "country place" leaves off and Petry's *Country Place* begins.

"Not truth but a distortion of it": *The Narrows*'s Monmouth, Connecticut

Like *The Street* and *Country Place, The Narrows* is concerned with the way multiple perspectives determine a community's identity. But rather than focus on the composite reality that emerges from many individual viewpoints, as *Country Place* does, Petry's third novel examines the ways that a community's identity evolves from the collaborative (and often combative) relationship between private opinions and public records. We come to know the Narrows, a black neighborhood that is increasingly segregated from the surrounding city of Monmouth, Connecticut, as an amalgam of individual perceptions and published accounts.[12] The viewpoints of Abbie Crunch, Link Williams, Malcolm Powther, and *Monmouth Chronicle* editor Peter Bullock are juxtaposed with stories and photographs in the *Chronicle* and the New York tabloids. While the press fails to capture the whole truth of the Narrows, it succeeds in altering the way people, both residents and outsiders, perceive the community.

It takes a peripheral character to recognize the role that newspapers have played in determining Link's fate: Miss Doris, Frances Jackson's voluble housekeeper, declares that the events leading to Link Williams's murder "were purely like a snowball and everybody give it a push, that twocent newspaper give it the last big push."[13] She is correct: The *Monmouth Chronicle*'s sensational articles on crime in the Narrows have indeed validated racism. The "white folks twocent newspaper" (415), as Miss Doris calls the *Chronicle,* has irresponsibly encouraged racial division to protect its own financial interests. But Miss Doris's important insight only hints at the extent that newspapers have affected Link Williams's relationship with Camilla Treadway Sheffield, a wealthy white woman from the other side of the city. In fact, newspaper articles and photos form a backdrop for their entire affair, from their first meeting in the Narrows to Link's eventual murder at Captain Bunny Sheffield's hands.

Camilla first comes to the Narrows, she explains to Link, because she has read a series of articles about the area in the *Monmouth Chronicle.* The stories about "the relationship between bad housing and crime" have piqued her curiosity, as have the accompanying "wonderful pictures" (62). Although her family lives in Monmouth, Camilla has apparently never visited this part of town before. Coming to the Narrows enables her to compare the images in the paper with reality, at least reality as she perceives it late at night in the fog. While Camilla meets Link because she is curious about the neighborhood portrayed in the paper, Link is available for a chance meeting with her because he is waiting for Jubine, the photographer, to return from a photo-shooting mission. Newspaper images and Jubine, the novel's most self-conscious image-maker, thus lead Link to his first encounter with Camilla.

Images and articles do more to break up the relationship than foster it, however. The newspaper as object plays a symbolic role in the breakup even before its words and pictures become an actively destructive force in the lovers' lives. When Abbie Crunch discovers her adopted son, Link, in bed with Camilla, she reacts to the young white woman's presence with cold fury: "She looked for something, anything, grabbed a newspaper, not even knowing what it was, brandishing it about the girl's head. 'Get out before I kill you'" (250). In a moment, however, the paper does not seem to be an entirely accidental choice of weapon. Abbie recalls spreading the *Monmouth Chronicle* around her late husband's chair when he was deathly ill; convinced he was merely drunk, she had been more intent on protecting her floors than tending to her mate. In that instance, the newspaper represented the censure of the community, at least the censure that Abbie believed the situation warranted. Angered by her husband's apparent drunkenness, she had worried that the white community of Monmouth would laugh at her behind her back: "The colored president of the white WCTU. A drunken husband. Well, he's colored. Ha-ha. Ha-ha. Ha-ha" (30). The local paper she spread on the floor had embodied the judgments that she believed would be passed on her and her husband.

Now, infuriated by her discovery of "a tramp" in bed with Link (253), Abbie invokes the community once again. She waves the rolled-up newspaper at Camilla, Link, and J.C., the little boy who has led Abbie to her horrifying discovery. The three of them have forced her to confront a situation she finds morally objectionable. Committed to defying white stereotypes of black people, Abbie lives her life according to a strict code of behavior. She is distressed by any display of emotion or physicality, especially in her own house, that suggests that blacks are less than strait-laced pillars of the community. Messy realities, such as her husband's illness and Link's affair with Camilla, contradict the fastidious image of morality that she has cultivated for herself. Abbie's waving of the newspaper symbolizes the power of the press and the power of the community sentiment that the press both mirrors and molds.

Although newspapers inevitably omit details and distill complicated stories into simple ones, they also provide readers with information they would not otherwise have. When such information confirms one's worst suspicions, the newspaper's rendering of truth can become a justification for prejudice against individuals and whole groups. Link is a perpetrator of such prejudice as well as a victim of it.

Given his imminent fate at the hands of newspaper journalists, Link is ironically quick to accept a New York tabloid's version of the "truth" about Camilla. The paper informs him that his Camilo Williams is actually Camilla Treadway Sheffield, the heiress to the Treadway Munitions fortune and the wife of Captain Bunny Sheffield. The stakes in his already-contentious relationship with Camilla immediately rise. Although he should be more skeptical, given his work as a Navy censor and his plans to become a historian, Link accepts the tabloid account at face value. Moreover, the article causes him to remember all of the racism and rejection he has experienced. He hastily lumps Camilla together with the long-ago teachers and employers who discriminated against him. The tabloid's portrayal of a conventionally married, predictably glamorous heiress wrecks his image of a mysterious, seemingly vulnerable woman—and his tenuous image of himself as an equal partner in the relationship. Perhaps just as important, the New York tabloid supplies him with the ammunition he needs to end a difficult affair, one that appears to have little future, regardless of Camilla's marital status. It gives him the material he needs to justify the hostility he has felt toward Camilla from the beginning.

Their troubles quickly multiply. Once Camilla has falsely charged Link with assaulting her, the brief news item that appears in the *Monmouth Chronicle* automatically transforms their private relationship into public property. From the perspective of Malcolm Powther, the Treadways' butler, we see the Treadways' domestic staff trying to reconcile their various images of Camilla with the newspaper's claim. They approach the tersely stated news item as a cryptic text inviting multiple interpretations. Just the thought of Camilla and Link together is enough to catalyze a multitude of anxieties about race, sex, class, and power.

Lest we come away with the impression that the *Monmouth Chronicle* is a voice without a face, Petry takes pains to describe Peter Bullock, the paper's editor, publisher, and owner. Bullock's doubts and weaknesses belie the newspaper's brash assertions of authority. Resentful of his wife's high standard of living (much like the Chandlers' standard in *The Street*), yet financially dependent on Treadway Munitions advertising dollars, committed to keeping the paper alive, yet willing to compromise its reputation, Bullock spends more time reacting subjectively to his various nemeses than acting objectively on the community's (or the newspaper's) behalf. He is repeatedly angered by Jubine, whose telling photographs seem staged: "The result was not truth but a distortion of it achieved by tricks of light, by special circumstance, surprise or shock" (365). But Bullock, hardly a slave to the truth, is so intimidated by Mrs. Treadway that he adjusts his news coverage to suit her demands.

Bullock quickly learns that he and the *Chronicle* are just as vulnerable to criticism as everybody written up in the paper: "Well, well, well," he says, "I always wondered what Public Opinion would look like in the flesh, and here he is: hatless, drunken, odoriferous, brandishing a New York tabloid about his head as though it were a weapon" (365). In an ironic parallel to Abbie's furious assault on Link and Camilla with a rolled-up paper, the anonymous visitor chastises Bullock for letting the community down. Waving the rival paper, he expresses a damning sentiment: "Things is in one hell of a shape when you got to read a New York paper to find out what's goin' on in your own home town" (366). In response, Bullock pulls out a gun—the only weapon powerful enough to vanquish the mighty hue and cry of "Public Opinion."

This showdown makes several important points. First, "Public Opinion" is not an amorphous, unseen mass but a flesh-and-blood individual, one of many who could invade Bullock's office and berate him. Second, "Public Opinion" has evidently accepted the New York tabloid's version of the accident story—that is, a story (by Jubine) that makes Camilla appear depraved and the Narrows appear mysterious, even magical. For lack of any competing image, other readers will likely accept the tabloid version as well. And finally, "Public Opinion" forces Bullock to realize that, as editor and publisher, he is only as strong as the images his paper presents. "Public Opinion" tells him, in no uncertain terms, that he has undermined his credibility as a community spokesman.

Spurred by Mrs. Treadway's demands, the *Chronicle*'s campaign against blacks climaxes with a much-embellished account of a black convict's escape and the publication of "a picture which showed the convict not as a man but as a black animal, teeth bared in a snarl, eyes crazy, long razor scar like a mouth" (377). Recalling the newspaper coverage of Bigger Thomas's escape in *Native Son,* the picture is used for such blatantly racist purposes that even Bullock feels ashamed. As the critic Vernon Lattin observes, "The *Monmouth Chronicle* has descended from an anti-slavery newspaper to a paper willing to portray Blacks as animals in order to please a patron."[14] Although the convict story has nothing to do with Link, the slanted account of the prisoner's escape (and his subsequent capture and death) creates the necessary context for Link's murder. The *Chronicle*'s readers have been, in effect, prepared for Link's violent death and urged to believe that such a murder is justifiable.

Chronicle readers expecting the paper's usual slant receive a surprise, however, in the paper's coverage of Link's murder and the police's apprehension of Bunny and Mrs. Treadway. The photo of Camilla's husband and mother sitting by the dock appears to be Jubine's handiwork. It shows the two suspects "sitting on the side of the road, near the dock, waiting, already under arrest, but waiting to be loaded into a police car, and people all around them, behind them, and there was horror and disbelief on the faces of all those people in the background" (413). For once, the city's most powerful white people are the object of censure. But in keeping with Jubine's previous photographs of the Narrows, the picture is more about universal pathos than the prejudices of the day. The image shows a frozen moment rather than the evolving dynamics of relationships within a community; it does not capture the whole truth because the whole truth keeps changing. Even so, the publication of the photo and accompanying news story (quoting Mrs. Treadway's attempts to cover up and finally rationalize her crime) are the latest installment in the *Chronicle*'s revisionary history of Monmouth. As the editor of that history, Bullock is motivated by his own needs—needs that may have little to do with the reporting of facts or the pursuit of the illusive truth.

As Monmouth's most pervasively public voice, the *Chronicle* is a medium for all kinds of bias as well as a record of it. The paper can erase an accident involving a prominent white woman; it can also create a climate in which everybody, black and white, fears blacks. But the paper's power is as illusory as the crime wave in the Narrows, since the bias of the news reflects Bullock's biases and vulnerabilities. In his relationships with his wife, Mrs. Treadway, the police chief, Jubine, his reporters, and "Public Opinion," among others, Bullock lives a life of negotiation and compromise rather than privilege and power. Just as his newspaper engages in an elaborate dialogue with the Monmouth citizens, so Bullock engages in a dialogue with other private citizens and other newspapers. The local paper is hardly the city's only public voice, however. In addition to the New York tabloids encroaching on Bullock's turf, Cesar the Writing Man and the Reverend Longworth (who uses a loudspeaker to proselytize on Dumble Street) also engage in a kind of call-and-response dialogue with the community.

Together, many different voices contribute to the cacophony that is Monmouth; many competing images contribute to our picture of Monmouth and the enclave known as the Narrows. I will argue in chapter 5 that while segregation and prejudice may threaten Monmouth's future (represented by the strong relationships or "links" between Link Williams and others in the town), the community is far from doomed. After Link's death, Abbie's willingness to befriend J. C. Powther illustrates Monmouth's best hope: new links between individuals who see beyond the stereotyping that inevitably constricts or "narrows" their vision of society and each other.

"He did not really belong in this all-white community": *Miss Muriel*'s Wheeling, New York

In size and appearance, Petry's Wheeling, as depicted in the stories in *Miss Muriel and Other Stories,* seems to be one and the same with her Lennox, Connecticut. The descriptions of Wheeling in "Miss Muriel," "The New Mirror," and "Has Anybody Seen Miss Dora Dean?" suggest that this small resort town, like Lennox, is based on Petry's native Old Saybrook. But whereas a sixty-five-year-old white male pharmacist narrates *Country Place,* the daughter of Wheeling's black pharmacist recounts the first three Wheeling stories. Petry thus brings her own experience even more directly to bear on these stories than on *Country Place.* And, while *Country Place*'s characters represent the shifting relationships between reality, illusion, and truth, the Wheeling characters do not seem yoked to any underlying philosophy. Petry's portrait of Wheeling emerges as a critique of American society. The town's faces may change, but the social prejudices remain constant in their powerful influence. As I discuss in chapter 6, Wheeling is a place where prejudices of race and gender determine relationships as well as individual personalities.

The descriptions of early twentieth-century Wheeling indicate that the town is, in many ways, an exceedingly pleasant place to live. Its natural beauty seems important in and of itself, not just as a foil for painful social truths. In "Miss Muriel," for instance, the narrator happily recounts a crabbing expedition with Uncle Johno and Dottle Smith: "The water in the creek was so clear I could see big crabs lurking way down on the bottom; I could see little pieces of white shells and beautiful stones. We didn't talk much while we were crabbing. Sometimes I lay flat on my stomach on the bridge and looked down into the water, watching the little eddies and whirlpools that formed after I threw my line in" (33). Although the activity in the creek obliquely foreshadows the conflicts awaiting the narrator and her companions, the passage mainly evokes a sense of shared peace and contentment. As one critic says of Petry's nature scenes: "[T]hey are reminders of the fact that the bleakness of life for black Americans has often been relieved by the simple pleasures of life—pleasures that other people enjoy."[15]

Another such scene in "The New Mirror" finds the narrator basking in the beauty of her family's backyard: "Though the sun was up, it was cool in the yard. The air was filled with a delicate fragrance that came from all the flowering shrubs, from the cherry blossoms and the pear blossoms, and from the small plants—violets and daffodils. A song sparrow was singing in the yard" (61). No matter what the Edenic imagery may preface, the specificity of the imagery suggests that the narrator and her family have experienced paradise in a way that Petry's impoverished Harlemites never have and never will. The tranquillity of the scene is unmistakable. Wheeling exudes a bucolic charm that does not come through in Petry's depictions of either Lennox or Lyme.

Petry is as concerned with the homes in Wheeling as she is with the Harlem tenements. The small-town dwellings, not surprisingly, prove to be much nicer than those of the ghetto. The shop where Mr. Bemish works, for instance, is a wonderfully inviting little place. Like the narrator's own home in the family pharmacy, the shoemaker's living quarters are in the back of his shop. Everything about Mr. Bemish's modest abode suggests a neat, appealingly spartan existence. The narrator's lengthy description of it reveals the fascination that the shoemaker's home holds for her: "Sometimes he forgets to draw the curtains that separate his sleeping quarters from the rest of the shop and I can see his bed. It is a brass bed. He evidently polishes it, because it shines like gold. It has a very intricate design on the headboard and the footboard. He has a little piece of flowered carpet in front of his bed. I can see his white china pot under the bed. A dark suit and some shirts hang on hooks on the wall" (5). Everything about Mr. Bemish's shop interests the narrator, perhaps because her home is similarly dedicated to comfort and order. Just talking to Bemish precipitates her proud description of her family's "turkey-red curtains" and their "old-fashioned sofa with a carved mahogany frame" (9, 10).

Although the narrator does not make the connection explicit, her family's pharmacy/home has much in common with Bemish's repair shop/home. To ensure the residents some privacy, both dwellings are divided into sections specifically for work and relaxation. But that privacy is illusory, since the narrator can easily gaze into Bemish's bedroom, and Aunt Sophronia's suitors can easily walk into the backyard behind the pharmacy. (Chink Johnson invades the parlor and plays the family piano; Chink, Dottle Smith, and Mr. Bemish all invade the backyard.) The blurring of boundaries within buildings deftly conveys the fact that people cannot entirely separate their public and private lives, nor can they always protect the sanctity of their homes.

The latter point is underscored by the story's conclusion. The bats that fly into the pharmacy one evening bring the competition between

Sophronia's suitors to a climax. While Mr. Bemish, the elderly white man, rushes to protect Sophronia from the startling invasion, Chink Johnson and Dottle Smith seem more interested in defending themselves. The general effect is pandemonium, and the narrator's subsequent spat with her even-tempered mother suggests that even their alliance is a tenuous one. The young narrator is so distracted by her own concerns, in fact, that she momentarily loses interest in Sophronia's warring suitors. When she catches up with Chink and Dottle at Bemish's shop, the shoemaker's home has been thrown into chaos as well.

The conflict that began at the narrator's drugstore/home thus plays itself out at Bemish's repair shop/home. The two black men can no longer tolerate the white man's presence. Through physical intimidation, Chink and Dottle succeed in frightening Mr. Bemish away from Sophronia. Though never entirely at ease with Bemish, the narrator seems genuinely dismayed by the breakup of his orderly household: "The inside of his shop looked very small and shabby and lonely. There wasn't anything left except his stove and he obviously couldn't take that" (56). In a few minutes, Bemish departs, along with his cat and a wagonload of possessions. The narrator sees that both his home and his place in the community have been easily wiped out—in effect, stricken from the map of Wheeling. The connection is left for the reader to make: If Bemish could be expelled from the community, so could the narrator's family, so could anyone.

While neither Bemish nor the narrator's parents evince the Chandlers' insatiable hunger for material goods, they share their wealthy counterparts' preference for aesthetically pleasing homes. A home in Wheeling is not the haven that the narrator would like it to be, however. Her family's privacy is just as vulnerable as Mr. Bemish's—a reality that the family must confront in both "Miss Muriel" and "The New Mirror." And, as is demonstrated in all of *Miss Muriel*'s small-town stories ("Doby's Gone," set in the fictional town of Wessex, Connecticut, as well as the Wheeling stories), nobody can remain completely impervious to the community's insinuations and intrusions.

Petry does not limit her vision of Wheeling to one time period. Both "Miss Muriel" and "The New Mirror" (originally published in 1963 and 1967, respectively) appear to be set in the 1920s. By contrast, "Has Anybody Seen Miss Dora Dean?" (1958) moves back and forth between the narrator's childhood and her present life three decades later; "The Migraine Workers" (1967) seems contemporary, as does "The Witness" (1970).[16] Approaching Wheeling from different points in time adds significantly to Petry's multifaceted depiction of the narrator's relationships with her family and town. We apprehend her as a grownup as well as a teenager and child; we can chart her maturation as a narrator, especially in "Has Anybody Seen Miss Dora Dean?" In that story, we can infer that the narrator's parents are dead; she has become, officially, the steward of family histories, both factual and imagined. As such, she is a much more self-conscious, artful narrator than she is in either "Miss Muriel" or "The New Mirror," tales that never leave the time or landscape of her Wheeling childhood.

In "The Migraine Workers" and "The Witness," Petry moves even farther away from the insular world of "Miss Muriel." These later stories emphasize the increasingly important roles in the community of both transportation and transience. As the owner of a truck stop, Pedro Gonzales of "The Migraine Workers" depends on travelers for his livelihood, but that does not mean he likes them. Quite the contrary, he is infuriated by the callousness of his transient customers, regardless of their color or social class. Charles Woodruff, the black high school teacher of "The Witness," experiences transience in a different way. A recent arrival in Wheeling, he does not tell anyone the real reason for his abrupt departure: his blindfolded "witnessing" of a gang rape. Despite his status as a financially secure, educated man, Woodruff cannot overcome the young white rapists' barbarous violence or ruthless prejudice. Their broken-down car, rough attire, and slang expressions mock his new station wagon, luxurious coat, and careful diction. Identified as the highly intelligent, though wayward, sons of Wheeling's upstanding citizenry, the boys symbolize the town's tenuous future—a future that will not include Woodruff, who is unable to confront and overcome his feelings of self-doubt and racial alienation.

Woodruff's exodus reveals both a lack of faith in his fellow townspeople and a profound lack of self-confidence. Because he is black and new to town, he considers himself a perennial outsider; he feels as if "he did not really belong in this all-white community" (213). Like the narrator of "The New Mirror," he does not expect fair play from white people, and his experience with the boys sufficiently justifies his cynicism. As I show in chapter 6, "The Witness" is Petry's most pessimistic portrait of Wheeling, providing a bleak contrast to the moments of naive happiness in "Miss Muriel" and "The New Mirror." Those stories' appealing scenes of Wheeling in spring and summer give way to snow and bitter cold in "The Witness." The humor that permeates all of the other Wheeling stories, furthermore, has no place in the telling of Woodruff's horrifying experience. The black teacher joins Lutie Johnson and Johnnie Roane in voluntarily leaving town. Like Lutie and Johnnie, Woodruff feels defeated by a community that had inspired ambivalence in him from the beginning. When he finds himself in a crisis, he believes driving away is the only alternative to staying behind and being crushed.

The Foundation of the Community: Relationships in Petry's Fiction

The care Petry takes to delineate towns and neighborhoods in all of her major works reveals the central importance of the community to her creative vision. Lyme and Harlem, Lennox and Wheeling, Monmouth and the Narrows—all are entities, complex characters, unto themselves. But Petry does not focus exclusively on the collective "character" of any given place. Her novels and her collection of short fiction also provide thorough renderings of human relationships, every community's social foundation.

The complexities of the relationships between individuals—the infinitely varied combinations of trust, prejudice, anxiety, love, anger, and fear—engage Petry's interest again and again. In the chapters that follow, I examine the personal relationships integral to Petry's conception of community in *The Street, Country Place, The Narrows,* and *Miss Muriel and Other Stories.* Petry's characters' ability (or inability) to confront prejudice and communicate clearly affects the quality of their relationships, shapes their perspectives of their home communities, and determines the overall health of those places. The connections (and disconnections) between individuals provide the basis for all of Petry's communities, Harlem as well as her New England towns.

Chapter Three

Fractured Friendships in *The Street*

The Street begins and ends on Harlem's 116th Street. As a character in its own right, 116th Street symbolizes the prejudices of race and gender that lithe, luckless Lutie Johnson cannot overcome, no matter how hard she tries. Lutie does not live on 116th Street alone, however. The street is home to an array of fellow strugglers: the malignant madam, Mrs. Hedges; the sexually obsessed building supervisor, Jones; his pathetic companion, Min; and Lutie's lonely eight-year-old son, Bub. The tenement they share belongs to an impoverished urban community whose residents are in frequent, if not necessarily friendly, contact with one another. In contrast with Richard Wright's *Native Son,* another naturalistic novel featuring a poor black protagonist struggling, futilely, against racism and sexism, *The Street* brings to life an entire community. Whereas *Native Son* focuses relentlessly on Bigger Thomas—who appears on virtually every page of the book—Petry's first novel explores the whole web of relationships making up Lutie's milieu.

Petry accomplishes this by entering not just Lutie's mind but the minds of Lutie's neighbors and son. She also includes sections identifying with Boots Smith, Lutie's would-be rapist, and Miss Rinner, Bub's third-grade teacher. As a result of the book's multiple perspectives, Keith Clark points out, "Petry's lens becomes more panoramic; other stories encroach upon Lutie's *mise-en-scène* and take on a tension and drama all their own."[1] The more we understand Lutie's history of fractured friendships and her place in the whole construct of relationships on 116th Street, the more we can understand her final, wrenching decision to leave Harlem—and her son—behind her.

The revelations about Lutie's past life in the novel's early chapters help explain her seemingly foolish decision to move to 116th Street. Lutie's family, first of all, offers her little help. Though she occasionally remembers her grandmother's advice, both her grandmother and mother are long dead. Her hard-drinking father is more of a liability than anything else. His raucous drinking parties quickly derail the foster-child enterprise that Lutie and her husband, Jim, run for a while. Lutie's attitude toward Pop mingles exasperation, embarrassment, and a small measure of pity. He seems content to live on the fringes of society, a place Lutie fully intends to leave behind.

Despite her objections to her father's way of life, however, Lutie turns to Pop for shelter after her marriage breaks up. Not surprisingly, she is repelled by the licentious atmosphere of the Harlem roominghouse that Pop shares with his latest girlfriend, Lil, and an assortment of other poor blacks. Most of her animosity focuses on Lil, an unambitious, unapologetically sensual woman. The thought of Lil's indoctrinating Bub into a sordid way of life provokes Lutie's rage. As uptight as she is upright, Lutie scorns the low-rent pleasures that Lil embraces: "[Lil] was always swallowing coffee in the kitchen; trailing through all seven rooms in housecoats that didn't quite meet across her lush, loose bosom; drinking beer in tall glasses and leaving the glasses in the kitchen sink so the foam dried in a crust around the rim—the dark red of her lipstick like an accent mark on the crust; lounging on the wide bed she shared with Pop and only God knows who else; drinking gin with the roomers until late at night" (10). Seen through Lutie's puritanical eyes, Lil is the personification of laziness and immorality. In other words, she is the opposite of all that Lutie imagines herself to be.

Even though Lil is a minor character who exists only in flashbacks, her briefly illuminated attitude toward Lutie deserves mention. Ironically, Lil appears to be just as concerned about Bub's welfare as Lutie is, only for different reasons: "Only last night Lutie slapped [Bub] so hard that Lil cringed away from her dismayed; her housecoat slipping even farther away from the fat curve of her breasts. 'Jesus!' she said. 'That's enough to make him deaf. What's the matter with you?'" (10–11). The rebuke suggests that Lil objects to Lutie's characteristically zealous approach to disciplining her young son. Thus the disapproval in this household is mutual: Lutie censures Lil for her loose morals, and Lil censures Lutie for being so hard on Bub.

Lutie's difficult relationships with Pop and Lil are not the only ones that have steered her toward 116th Street. Her past relationship with Mrs. Chandler of Lyme, Connecticut, plays just as crucial a role in her decision to set out on her own with Bub. Like Lil and Pop, Mrs. Chandler exists only in narrative flashbacks. But it is clear that this self-absorbed young white woman and her household remain important to Lutie.

In the flashbacks we see that Lutie is acutely aware of Mrs. Chandler's every move and word. Although Mrs. Chandler seems "awfully nice" on the surface (40), Lutie notes significant lapses in her employer's behavior.

Not only does Mrs. Chandler avoid her young son and cheat on her husband, she refuses to acknowledge Lutie as a person in her own right. Lutie is particularly hurt by the way Mrs. Chandler condescends to her in public. When the two women part company at the end of a companionable train ride, Lutie recalls: "There was a firm note of dismissal in [Mrs. Chandler's] voice so that the other passengers pouring off the train turned to watch the rich young woman and her colored maid: a tone of voice that made people stop to hear just when it was the maid was to report back for work" (51). Because their relationship is based on the white woman's power and the black woman's subservience, Mrs. Chandler cannot resist asserting her control, while Lutie cannot help feeling resentful. Desperately in need of a friend, Lutie realizes with painful clarity that Mrs. Chandler will never view her as anything but a loyal servant.

By the end of her two-year stint in Lyme, Lutie is so preoccupied with her own problems that she cannot see that Mrs. Chandler, in her own way, is just as lonely and frustrated as she is. Mrs. Chandler's endless parties and affairs do not erase anxiety or replace a loveless marriage. Like Lutie, Mrs. Chandler seems reluctant to sustain intimacy with anyone, except perhaps her domineering mother. Had they been able to communicate as equals, these two young women might have helped each other. But when Mrs. Chandler finally reaches out to Lutie (who has returned home to Jamaica only to find Jim living with another woman), the acknowledgment is too little, too late. It is merely an expression of regret that Lutie is no longer available to perform her usual labors: "Mrs. Chandler wrote her a long letter and Jim forwarded it from Jamaica. '*Lutie dear: We haven't had a decent thing to eat since you left. And Little Henry misses you so much he's almost sick*————' She didn't answer it. She had more problems than Mrs. Chandler and Little Henry had and they could always find somebody to solve theirs if they paid enough" (55).

Lutie's brusque thoughts reveal the extent of her disaffection. She knows how unhappy the Chandlers are, but she does not allow herself to care about any of them, even Little Henry. If Mrs. Chandler had admitted that she, not just her son, missed Lutie, or if she had expressed concern for Lutie and Bub, maybe Lutie would have reacted to the letter differently. But Mrs. Chandler cannot turn the key in her own or Lutie's locked heart; the excerpt from her letter contains no direct revelation of sympathy to which Lutie could respond in kind. As a result, Lutie abruptly ends her relationship with Mrs. Chandler. Now that she has acquired the materialistic Chandlers' unswerving devotion to the

American dream—and all of what Toni Morrison calls "that term's elu-
sive mixture of hope, realism, materialism, and promise"[2]—Lutie is
determined to succeed on her own, free of the oppressive restrictions
placed on her in Lyme.

Lutie's marriage is no more successful or satisfactory than any of her
other relationships. Having married Jim when she was seventeen, Lutie
has seen her "big handsome husband" lose his self-esteem along with his
job (41). Perennially unemployed and apparently uninterested in the foster children who account for a small income, he cajoles Lutie into going
out at night when Lutie knows they should stay home with the children.
Later, when Lutie is offered the job in Lyme, Jim reacts with sullen taci-
turnity. The marriage is in trouble, and Lutie is destined to be the last to
know. Mrs. Pizzini, the grocer who provides Lutie with a job reference,
warns her early on, "It's best that the man do the work when the babies
are young. And when the man is young. Not good for the woman to
work when she's young. Not good for the man" (33). But Lutie does not
have a choice. The job in Lyme will pay the bills in Jamaica; the fact that
she has to leave her family to provide them shelter is an irony she cannot
alter or overcome.

It is only after Pop informs her that Jim is *carrying on with another
woman* that Lutie makes an unannounced visit to Jamaica (52). Her
long absences, combined with Jim's excess free time, have led to the
inevitable: an affair with another woman right under the roof Lutie has
paid for. By the time she confronts Jim with his betrayal, he is too
demoralized to care what his wife thinks: "He only shrugged and
laughed. That was all she could get out of him—laughter" (54).
Although Lutie eventually sympathizes with Jim's concomitant loss of
morale and morality, she sees no immediate reason to salvage the marriage. Having long ago lost his dignity, Jim will not allow her to reclaim
her own: "If even once he had put his arms around her and said he was
sorry and asked her to forgive him, she would have stayed. But he
didn't" (54).

Lutie's most intimate relationship with another adult has therefore
ended before her arrival on 116th Street. She cannot afford a divorce, so
she is still legally bound to Jim. More important, they are both bound to
a racist society that seems bent on destroying the black family. Although
nobody forces Jim to commit adultery or Lutie to leave him for doing so,
the turn of events is hardly surprising. The couple's extenuating financial
circumstances and breakdown in communication were creating problems
even before Lutie left for Lyme. In a series of painful insights near the

novel's conclusion, Lutie views the failure of her marriage in starkly economic terms:

> The women work because the white folks give them jobs—washing dishes and clothes and floors and windows. The women work because for years now the white folks haven't liked to give black men jobs that paid enough for them to support their families. And finally it gets to be too late for some of them. Even wars don't change it. The men get out of the habit of working and the houses are old and gloomy and the walls press in. And the men go off, move on, slip away, find new women. Find younger women. (389)

Thus Lutie perceives that racism does much more than afflict individual blacks; it also erodes their relationships. Lutie's revelations provide a social frame for the failure of her marriage and suggest, further, that sexual politics are inextricably bound to race relations. As Jim's wife, her ability to find employment enabled them to keep their house; her inability to hold a job and simultaneously perform the traditional duties of wife and mother, however, caused Jim to leave her for another woman. Understanding her no-win situation does not make things any easier for Lutie. Nor does her uncompromising approach to relationships bring her any comfort. Empathy is a luxury Lutie cannot afford; she is too preoccupied with survival to give much thought to other people's troubles.

Lutie's Self-Exile on 116th Street

When a cold November wind propels Lutie toward a fresh set of relationships on 116th Street, she is hardly predisposed to trust any new acquaintances, no matter who they are. She has so much experience in aborted, unhappy relationships that the prospect of a welcoming community never even occurs to her. In contrast, the potential problems posed by Mrs. Hedges, Jones, and Min spring quickly to her mind: Mrs. Hedges makes her feel violated; Jones poses an obvious sexual threat; and the toothless, whispering Min is an appalling specter of submission. But Lutie is so eager to leave behind her old home that she temporarily pushes aside all of her amply justified anxieties. After recoiling from each of her new neighbors in turn, she decides (with what may appear willful perversity) to ignore her intuitive feelings of discomfiture and outright danger. Like a fugitive slave, she concentrates on the mechanics of escape and day-to-day survival rather than future prospects. She will embark on a journey with only the vaguest destination: financial and psychological freedom.

Long before she runs away from Harlem for good, it seems, Lutie is rehearsing her final departure. Her failure to connect meaningfully with people breeds dissatisfaction and distrust in her, and she feels increasing apprehension each time a new relationship teeters on the verge of intimacy. Because her desire to start over exceeds her ability to settle down, she is always packing up and moving on. An escape artist by nature, she tells herself that "With the apartment Bub would be standing a better chance, for he'd be away from Lil" (26). Just as significant, Lutie herself will be away from the dreaded Lil.

As her life at the tenement unfolds, however, we see that Lutie will not be able to control her destiny on 116th Street any better than she could in the seedy boardinghouse. Try as she might, she cannot always maintain an icy distance from her fellow tenants, nor can she prevent them from consorting with each other. As usual, Lutie finds herself in a web of relationships, each of which involves a complex interplay of race, sexuality, and power. Other people's fates impinge on Lutie's own, despite her efforts to remain free of entanglements.

Mrs. Hedges as the Street Personified

From the beginning, Lutie views Mrs. Hedges as a nemesis—and with good reason. Intelligent, industrious, and willing to wield the power available to her, Mrs. Hedges is much more of a threat to Lutie than the lazy Lil would have been. As the madam of a prostitution ring, Mrs. Hedges has co-opted the system that is quickly closing in on Lutie. Whereas Lutie expresses shocked outrage every time a man makes a sexual advance on her, Mrs. Hedges calmly recognizes male lust as an opportunity to turn a profit. Her long scrutiny of the street has taught her that footloose young black men are much more reliable as customers than as husbands. Like the Chandlers, she is a capitalist who worships at the altar of supply and demand.

Exploitation of women is essential to Mrs. Hedges's business. If every man who passes her window is a potential customer, then every pretty young woman is potential merchandise. Even though she occasionally evinces sympathy for other black women—Min, for example—she typically views them as sexual commodities rather than fellow strugglers. This is evident every time she addresses Lutie Johnson, whom she repeatedly invites into prostitution.

As Junto's business partner, Mrs. Hedges functions as the white power broker's eye on Harlem. She understands the community's

oppressed, anguished mind, and her insights fuel Junto's business success. It is Mrs. Hedges who advises Junto to invest in nightclubs, bars,
and prostitution houses. Such businesses provide a temporary escape for
racially subjugated patrons who take their small pleasures wherever they
can find them. Mrs. Hedges does not seem to feel that she is betraying
her race by exposing black people's areas of vulnerability to Junto.
Intent on her own survival, she sees her alliance with Junto as a means of
securing a position of authority in the community. At least in relation to
other blacks, she has abdicated her role as vulnerable black female and
assumed the mantle of powerful white male.

Mrs. Hedges's predatory gaze and her sexually ambiguous appearance
immediately establish her status as 116th Street's surrogate oppressor.
On first sight, Lutie is repelled by Mrs. Hedges's flat, snake-like eyes
"wandering over her body, inspecting and appraising her from head to
foot" (6). Like the cold wind that leaves Lutie feeling "naked and bald"
(2), Mrs. Hedges's intrusive gaze makes Lutie feel sexually vulnerable.
The more Lutie looks at Mrs. Hedges, the more disturbed she is by the
older woman's intimidating demeanor. Large, muscular, and seemingly
oblivious to the freezing weather, Mrs. Hedges has an androgynous, oth-
erworldly appearance about her. To Lutie, she looks like a "snake
charmer" (19)—a characterization that is both masculine and malevo-
lent. The older woman's turban complements the impression of mystical
power created by her penetrating stare. Even her name evokes a troubling ambiguity: The courtesy title "Mrs." ironically insists on a marital
status she does not have, while "Hedges" alludes to her business acumen
(she "hedges her bets" by preying on vulnerable blacks) and her ambiguous conversation (she hedges the unsavory subject of prostitution while
intimating that Lutie should give it a try).

Despite all the evidence to the contrary, Mrs. Hedges and Lutie have
more in common than either can admit. Like Lutie, Mrs. Hedges is
extremely vulnerable behind her armor of self-sufficient strength. While
Lutie may feel bald, Mrs. Hedges *is* bald. In a section written from her
perspective, we learn that Mrs. Hedges wears her trademark turban to
hide the affliction brought on by a terrible fire. She believes that her
physical deformity has ruined her chances at love and intimacy: "Scarred
like this, hair burned off her head like this, she would never have any
man's love. She never would have had it, anyway, she thought realistically. But she could have bought it. This way she couldn't even buy it"
(246). Although in word and deed Junto attempts to win Mrs. Hedges
over, she refuses to believe his attentions are anything except the admi-

ration "he would have for another man—a man he regarded as his equal" (246). Like Lutie, Mrs. Hedges wants to see without being seen: "When the nurses and doctors bent over her to change the dressings, she watched them with hard, baleful eyes, waiting for the moment when they would expose all the ugliness of her burnt, bruised body. They couldn't conceal the expressions on their faces. Sometimes it was only a flicker of dismay, and then again it was sheer horror, plain for anybody to see—undisguised, uncontrollable" (246–47).

Mrs. Hedges's appearance, like Lutie's, is the bane of her existence. In the eyes of the public, one woman is an object of revulsion, the other of lust. Neither can escape society's warping tunnel vision, which inevitably shapes their own perceptions and reactions. Whereas Lutie reacts by silently railing against the people around her, slapping her son, and finally killing Boots Smith, Mrs. Hedges reacts by resolving to accept the rules of the game—and play them to her advantage. If she cannot have love, she will have money. And money will give her the power to join the ranks of men. She will be subject rather than object; she will possess the street and all its inhabitants with her hard, flat gaze.

Since each imposes sexist stereotypes on the other, the bridge between Lutie and Mrs. Hedges cannot be crossed. Mrs. Hedges's "if you can't beat 'em, join 'em" philosophy is at best an unpleasant compromise. She denies herself the possibility of a relationship with Junto, who appears to love her; she profits from the exploitation of vulnerable women and desperate men; and she contributes to the alienation and disaffection of proud young women like Lutie Johnson. In the end, she subjects Lutie to the same harsh treatment that has crippled her own life.

Lutie, however, is no kinder in her treatment of Mrs. Hedges. Far from recognizing the older woman as a fellow victim of a sexist, racist society, she responds to her with the same revulsion that Mrs. Hedges has come to expect from men put off by her appearance: "She put her hand on Mrs. Hedges's shoulder. The flesh under the flannel of the gown was hard. The muscles bulged. And she took her hand away, repelled by the contact" (240). Lutie's rare gesture of intimacy sets off a rapid chain of events: She pulls back because Mrs. Hedges's body is as hard as a man's; Mrs. Hedges experiences a quickly withdrawn touch signaling physical revulsion; and finally Mrs. Hedges stereotypes Lutie, once again inviting her into prostitution. Sexism thus conditions these women's responses and forestalls friendship or any kind of mutual support.

The insurmountable gap between Lutie and Mrs. Hedges is most apparent at the novel's end. Because Lutie has no trustworthy friends to consult after Bub has been caught stealing letters, she believes the white lawyer who says she must pay him $200 to handle the case. At this point, she thinks of people who might lend her the money: her father, Lil, the women she works with. The first two she rejects because she knows they will not have the money; the last group, she does not know well enough to ask. Mrs. Hedges would be a possibility, but she never even crosses Lutie's mind. To her, Mrs. Hedges is an enemy, not an ally. For her part, Mrs. Hedges (who knows Bub has been incarcerated) is not about to volunteer assistance to a haughty young beauty who does not yet know her place. The standoff between the two women is especially unfortunate since Mrs. Hedges appears to be the only person capable of influencing the actions of Junto, who in turn influences Boots Smith. Mrs. Hedges might have been able to prevent, or at least alter, the final encounter between Boots, Junto, and Lutie had Lutie asked her to intervene.

A Minimal Existence on Society's Margins

Whereas Lutie sees Mrs. Hedges as a threat to her scrupulously maintained privacy, Min sees Lutie as a threat to her relationship with Jones. Min leads a nomadic existence, moving in with one man after another, apparently for the shelter they can provide as much as for any kind of love or companionship. Toothless and broken down, she has neither Mrs. Hedges's entrepreneurial savvy nor Lutie's youthful strength. When we first come upon her, she is pathetically dependent on Jones, cruel and crazy though he may be. For all her weaknesses, however, Min is not without hope or resolve. Although she has always been dependent on men for shelter, she finally realizes that her degraded life with Jones is hardly a life at all. Her neatly executed escape from their apartment is an effective response to his furious silences, his physical abuse, and his sexual obsession with Lutie Johnson.

Ironically, Min believes that her newfound courage comes from another black man, the Prophet David, whose claims to mystical power attract the city's unhappy, powerless black women. His name suggesting "profit" as well as prophecy, this urban conjurer feeds off the oppression imposed on women by his fellow black men. The women who come to him seek vicarious authority, permission to take control of their lives, and the consolation of believing that at least one man takes them seriously. The Prophet serves a priestly function in these women's lives, but he is a secular priest who offers no redemption beyond that day's purchase of potions and powder.

Min, too naive and desperate to question the Prophet David's claim to supernatural power, responds gratefully to his calm listening. Although she must pay for the Prophet's time and the voodoo props and powders that he recommends (and thus deprive herself a while longer of the false teeth she needs), she believes that the expense is well worth it. Her contact with the Prophet eventually enables her to emancipate herself from Jones. For the first time, she leaves a man of her own volition instead of waiting until he throws her out.

Uneducated and simple though she may be, Min finds comfort and possibility in Harlem, whereas Lutie finds only hostility and a series of dead ends. As Marjorie Pryse sees it, "Petry clearly offers Min's alternatives, if not Min herself as models for Lutie. How might the novel, and Lutie's life, have been different, for example, had she gone to the Prophet David for help when Bub is arrested instead of the white lawyer who wants to charge her two hundred dollars? Might the Prophet have been able to tell her she didn't need a lawyer?"[3] Very likely the Prophet would be more sympathetic than the white lawyer whose services Lutie distractedly seeks. But it is Mrs. Hedges, not the Prophet, who initially makes Min's empowerment possible. She is the one who tells Min the Prophet's name and address and then cautions: "And if I was you, dearie, I wouldn't let him see them bills all at one time. Root doctor or not, he's probably jest as hungry as you and me" (120). Although she is clearly uncomfortable in the role of advisor, Mrs. Hedges provides the information requested of her and declines Min's offer of payment.

Mrs. Hedges thus responds graciously to the other woman's obvious trust in her. Her guidance, freely given, opens the door to a source of commiseration and affirmation and inspires Min to new generosity: "Riding toward 116th Street on the bus, she decided that every time she heard about some poor woman in trouble she would send her to the Prophet David. He was so easy to talk to, his eyes were so kind, and he knew his business. Seeing as Mrs. Hedges had been responsible for her finding him, she really ought to do something in return" (137). Min is therefore revitalized, thanks to the aid of two professional exploiters of women: Mrs. Hedges, who runs a prostitution house, and the mercenary Prophet, who sells supposedly magical powders and potions. Significantly, she never considers the possibility that women might help each other directly. But having acquiesced to the masculine madam and the profit-seeking prophet, she is still better able than Lutie to shape her own destiny.

When Min eventually decides to leave Jones and the 116th Street tenement, she again relies on Mrs. Hedges's assistance. Mrs. Hedges finds her a pushcart man who will facilitate a clandestine departure. Min immediately sees the pushcart man as husband material: "Now this was a strong man and about her age from the wiry gray hair near his temples; willing to work, too, for this work he was doing was hard" (370–71). She weighs not only his physical strength but also his ability to make money and to intimidate landlords: "If he was a strong man like this one, they were afraid to talk roughly" (371). Love, evidently, is not an issue for Min. She is looking for vicarious strength (like that which she purchased from the Prophet), since "a woman living alone really didn't stand much chance" (371). She accepts sexism as her due and gamely figures it into her plans.

Unlike Lutie, Min does not expect to be treated fairly or even as an adult, and on the rare occasions when she is, her response is amazed pleasure. Her weary, degraded life is lit by only occasional moments of energizing hope. Lutie's life, by contrast, consists of many high hopes repeatedly dashed by social degradation. Neither character, in fact, has much reason for hope. As Barbara Christian observes, "Nowhere [in *The Street*] is there relief from bleakness—not in the personalities of the people or the institutions of the community. Even the spiritualists have turned commercial, and the bars have become dangerous" (Christian, 64). Min expects injustice and celebrates the few victories that come her way; Lutie expects justice and reels in fury each time her dreams are crushed. Both women are so beaten down by circumstance that they can barely imagine the healing effects of generosity, except as it applies to their own needs. Even Min, who vows to help other women locate the Prophet, does not seem likely to come into frequent contact with those who might benefit from her counsel. Forced to look out for herself at all times, she has little opportunity—or impetus—to look out for others as well.

A "Super" Madman

Although neither Mrs. Hedges nor Min becomes a role model for Lutie, Jones quickly becomes a father figure for Bub. The emotionally disturbed building superintendent uses Bub as a means of exacting revenge on Lutie, whom he loathes once she eludes his attempted rape. He devises a letter-stealing scheme that will get Bub in trouble with the law and set Lutie on her disastrous collision course with Boots Smith and Junto.[4] That he can think up such a plot suggests that he is clever, despite the impression of plodding ineptness he initially makes. The combination of sly intelligence and sexual depravity is exceedingly dangerous; thus, Lutie's early suspicions about him are quickly confirmed.

Seen through Lutie's eyes, Jones is a monstrosity deserving no pity. Yet Petry humanizes Jones by sketching his wretched past and writing from his perspective as well as Lutie's. We discover that Jones has a history of jobs that have removed him from society: He has worked in isolation on ships and as the cellar-dwelling superintendent in a series of rundown apartment buildings. With each passing year, he has grown more peculiar and more starved for female companionship. In his own way, then, Jones is just as much of a victim as the women he abuses. His degrading jobs have made him pathologically lonely. Even in Harlem, where he is hardly alone, he cannot find anyone to fill the terrible chasm of his needs.

By the time that Jones has assaulted Lutie, his sexual dysfunction has outstripped his sanity. He is so disconnected from society that he cannot separate fiction from fact. After Mrs. Hedges thwarts the attempted rape, he does not reconsider the wisdom of stalking his young tenant. On the contrary, his failure heightens his monomaniacal interest in Lutie. Only now, he believes that she is his worst enemy. Having decided that Lutie "was in love with the white man, Junto, and she couldn't bear to have a black man touch her" (281), he imagines himself as the innocent object of Lutie's cruel scorn:

> He tortured himself with the picture of them lying naked in bed together, possibly talking about him, laughing at him. He attempted to put words into their mouths.
>
> "Can you imagine, Mr. Junto, that Jones making love to me?"
>
> He couldn't get any further than that because his mind refused to stay still. It seemed to have become a livid, molten, continually moving, fluid substance in his brain that spewed up fragments of thought until his head ached with the effort to follow the motion, to analyze the thoughts. (281)

Jones's thoughts are not just comically grotesque; they are yet another revelation of the ways that race and sexuality are inextricably bound. In Jones's deranged mind, Lutie's rejection of his sexual overtures is due solely to his color. The perceived racial slight fuels his demented rage; his revenge on Lutie will also be his response to a lifetime of racial subjugation. He is not angry just at her but at the whole mainstream culture that argues for the preeminence of white men over black men. Victim turned persecutor, he exercises what he considers the one power play available to him: the corruption of Lutie's child. Given his mental state, it is no surprise that Jones never worries that he may be wrecking another black male's life. He is incapable of thinking rationally about relationships or other people's lives; he is interested only in hurting others as a means of assuaging his own pain.

Boots as Oppressor-Turned-Victim

Lutie's other would-be rapist, Boots Smith, is also trapped in a matrix of sexual and racial relations, a matrix that sets up his assault on Lutie and precipitates his death. A talented musician indebted to Junto for his job as bandleader, Boots seems as coldly rational as Jones does feverishly irrational. The section of the book told from his point of view reveals that he is a bitter man repelled by the thought of black men fighting what he considers a white man's war. He has successfully eluded the draft to serve in World War II, but he cannot elude the fact that he owes his career to Junto. No matter how disgusted he may be by his dependence on a white man, he has become so cynical that he barely considers contesting Junto's claim to Lutie. He knows that appropriating her will end his career as a musician: "Balance Lutie Johnson. Weigh Lutie Johnson. Long legs and warm mouth. Soft skin and pointed breasts. Straight slim back and small waist. Mouth that curves over white, white teeth. Not enough. She didn't weigh enough when she was balanced against a life of saying 'yes sir' to every white bastard who had the price of a Pullman ticket. Lutie Johnson at the end of a Pullman run. Not enough. One hundred Lutie Johnsons didn't weigh enough" (265).

To befriend Lutie, to court her honorably, would be to lose his tenuous foothold in a white man's world. He will not give up the money and prestige he has attained, attributes his color would ordinarily have denied him. His subsequent dealings with Lutie reflect both his unwillingness to relinquish his vicarious power and his own feelings of racial subjugation.

But, like Jones, Boots wants to get even with Junto and the white patriarchy that Junto represents. Unable or unwilling to confront his adversary directly, he decides to seize sexual possession of Lutie, the object of Junto's interests. When he tries to assault Lutie, he is thinking more about Junto than his victim: "Sure, Lutie would sleep with Junto, but he was going to have her first. . . . Yeah, he can have the leavings. After all, he's white and this time a white man can have a black man's leavings" (423). Victimizing a woman of his own race emerges as the pervasive black male response to racial subjugation in *The Street*. Boots's death at Lutie's hands underscores both the horror and the futility of such an action. Combat between black male and black female does nothing to lessen the racism that both genders have suffered.

Junto as Neighborhood Villain

In Petry's Harlem, Junto personifies all that is white, male, and evil. He is the novel's most obvious candidate for villain, and his shadowy presence guarantees a horrific end to Lutie's life in Harlem.[5] He owns the tenement where she lives. He is in league with Mrs. Hedges, who tries to talk Lutie into a life of prostitution. He controls Boots Smith, whose frustration manifests itself in hostility toward Lutie. He is present when Lutie comes to Boots's apartment in desperate pursuit of $200. He is first in line for sexual favors when Boots tells Lutie how she can obtain the money she needs. He figures prominently in Boots's decision to rape Lutie. Finally, he is in Lutie's mind as she strikes her first blows against Boots.

In spite of all this damning evidence against him, even Junto appears to have a grain of humanity. We learn, for instance, that Junto recognized Mrs. Hedges's potential in a way that nobody else, black or white, ever had. His conversations with her reveal that he is capable of admiration and tenderness, perhaps even love. Had Mrs. Hedges been able to accept Junto's affections, maybe he would not have pursued Lutie Johnson at all. But the adult relationships as they exist in *The Street* allow for little trust and even less love. As the supreme agent of racism, Junto is also an object of the hateful prejudice that he embodies. For all of his power, he is far from a happy person. The two women he is interested in—Mrs. Hedges and Lutie—are both black, and neither of them is willing to suffer his attentions. Furthermore, Lutie's attack on Boots and her subsequent departure from Harlem spell failure for Junto as well as the parties directly involved. Junto loses his star bandleader—and his chance to quench his desire for Lutie. A white power broker in a black community, Junto (who always seems to be sitting alone) is as alienated from his immediate environment as his black victims are from the society at large.

Miss Rinner the Tormented Sinner

Junto is not the novel's only white character who acquires some dimension. Miss Rinner, the white woman who teaches Bub's third-grade class in Harlem, also emerges as an unhappy object of racism as well as a perpetrator of it. Although Miss Rinner has the professional status and independence Lutie desires, she is no more pleased with her situation than Lutie is. In fact, she lives in fear of the children she teaches in Harlem.

The white teacher's section illustrates the presence of racism in the public schools and delineates Bub's life away from home. Bub is one among many anonymous children whose collective odor fills Miss Rinner with revulsion: "As the years slipped by—years of facing a room swarming with restless children—she came to think of the accumulation of scents in her classroom with hate as 'the colored people's smell,' and then finally as the smell of Harlem itself—bold, strong, lusty, frightening" (328). Even though the first three adjectives are positive, the scent nevertheless frightens Miss Rinner, who recoils from her students' physical presence.

Her undisguised loathing inevitably makes her a destructive presence in the classroom. In her mind, she is not there to teach children, but to police an unruly horde. She begins each week filled with unspent emotions from weeks past: "And when the class assembled, the sight of their dark skins, the sound of the soft blurred speech that came from their throats, filled her with the hysterical desire to scream. As the week wore along, the desire increased, until by Fridays she was shaking, quivering inside" (329). When the narrative perspective shifts away from Miss Rinner to Bub, we can understand why he fibs to escape class early, why he has already turned to the streets for his education.

Miss Rinner is not a simplistically drawn tyrant, however. She is also a victim of racism, since her students' poverty and limited future impede her ability to teach them effectively. She cannot erase their hunger, their ragged clothes, or their disregard for white teachers. The hopelessness of her task fills her with bottomless fear. She is a lonely white woman whose hostility barely hides her defining emotion of terror. The smell of her students is "frightening" (328). The children themselves "frightened her. Their parents and Harlem itself frightened her" (330). They bring penknives to school (not exactly murder weapons, but nevertheless terrifying to Miss Rinner), and she tries desperately to switch schools: "Ten years had gone by and she was still here, and the fear in her had now reached the point where even the walk to the subway from the school was a terrifying ordeal" (331). So she huddles near other white people at the train station, "taking refuge in their nearness—refuge from the terror of these black people" (331), and then she returns the next morning to the school where the children's sullen expression "never failed to infuriate her at the same time that it frightened her" (333).

Miss Rinner, then, is a kind of photographic negative of Lutie. She is a white minority working in a black community; Lutie is a black minority living in a white country. Miss Rinner hates blacks, Lutie hates whites. Yet both are single women supporting themselves, and neither has any viable recourse for her pent-up emotions. The world is closing in on Miss Rinner just as quickly and cruelly as it is on Lutie. Both are being confined, hardened, and irrevocably alienated by the pervasive influence of racism. Ironically, these rather similar women, though linked by Bub, will never even cross paths. Miss Rinner would never think of visiting a student's home and establishing a rapport with his mother, and Bub is caught stealing long before Lutie can take a day off and visit his classroom.

Bigger Thomas in the Making?

Eight-year-old Bub is the novel's most moving example of a black male victimized by poverty, corruption, and deceit. In the sections written from Bub's perspective, we see that he is a lonely, fearful child who desperately needs Lutie's time and attention. When Lutie dresses herself for an appearance with Boots Smith's band, for instance, Bub wrestles with his emotions: "He didn't want her to know that he was afraid to stay in the house alone. He wished there was some way he could keep her with him without telling her he was scared" (211). He hides his feelings from her because he does not want to add to her worries or risk her anger. Lutie, for her part, is too preoccupied with her new career prospects to worry about Bub's immediate fears. She does not realize the extent of his vulnerability or the direct correlation between his actions and his love for her.

Both of Bub's attempts to please his mother backfire. When he sets up a shoeshine stand, with Jones's help, in an honest effort to earn money, Lutie reacts to his enterprise by slapping him violently. To her, it appears that Bub has embraced a racist stereotype. Her thoughts reveal that her misdirected anger stems from fear: "[Y]ou're afraid that if he's shining shoes at eight," she tells herself, "he will be washing windows at sixteen and running an elevator at twenty-one, and go on doing that for the rest of his life. And you're afraid that this street will keep him from finishing high school; that it may do worse than that and get him into some kind of trouble that will land him in reform school because you can't be home to look out for him because you have to work" (67). She is angry at society, not at him, but this distinction vanishes as soon as she strikes him. Her attempt to explain her anger heightens Bub's awareness of her frustrated unhappiness without wiping away the violence of her reaction. Bub, too, is frustrated because he does not yet understand that a few extra dollars will not release him or Lutie from the grips of racism. Like Lutie, he is convinced that money will set them free.

His second attempt to earn money fails even more miserably than the first. Because Jones ingeniously couches the letter-stealing scheme in terms of the cops-and-robbers movies that Bub favors, Bub believes that the police actually sanction his thefts and accepts some of the money Jones finds in the envelopes as payment for his good work. By committing a federal offense, Bub plays right into Jones's hands. He is helping Jones exact revenge on Lutie, who refuses to return the superintendent's maniacal affections. When Bub is arrested and taken to a detention center, the situation is a much harsher rendition of the shoeshine episode. Once again, Bub does not know what he has done wrong or why he is being punished so severely. And once again, Lutie is too distraught to clarify matters very much. Her final, unexplained departure leaves Bub in suspended helplessness. Having been privy to his loneliness in the pitch-black apartment ("It made him feel as though he were left hanging in space and that he couldn't know how much space there was other than that his body occupied" [215]), we can easily imagine Bub's mounting terror in the detention center, once he realizes that Lutie is not ever coming back for him. He is Bigger Thomas in miniature, an emblem of the hardships that economically deprived black males face.

A Complex Web of Flawed Characters

Lutie's character is deepened and made more complex by the presence of other characters, both male and female, who in their frustration and vulnerability are like her but in their expressions of these emotions quite different. We come to see Lutie as one flawed, intricate character among many. Naturalistic details—the filthy street, the ferocious wind, and the dark, depressing rooms of Lutie's apartment—heighten the effect of the novel's human characterization without overwhelming it. While Lutie and the others are obviously affected by their oppressive environment, as characters traditionally are in naturalistic works, they also play significant roles in perpetuating that environment. Lutie's sometimes harsh treatment of her son, Mrs. Hedges's calculated evaluations of others, Min's pathetic timidity, Jones's insane pursuit of Lutie, and even Bub's naive willingness to steal contribute to their community's collective state of frustration.

Nellie Y. McKay points out that Lutie is not a cardboard "victim of her social environment,"[6] since all of the characters in this novel appear to contribute at least obliquely to each other's doom. Lutie is a poignant figure partly because for so long she refuses to believe that she is fighting a losing battle. Even after Bub's arrest, she hopes that $200 will turn her own and her son's lives around. Such an unthinking assumption is her downfall. Like two of American literature's most famous self-made men—Fitzgerald's Gatsby and Faulkner's Sutpen in *Absalom, Absalom!*—she repeatedly sees herself as immune to obligation to others.

Lutie attempts to achieve her goals without considering how her behavior will affect other people or how they will react to her. Her determination is integral to this novel of social determinism. Yet, like Gatsby and Sutpen, she is strangely innocent of the ways of the world, and, as McKay observes, her innocence leads to her failure (McKay, 135). Lutie believes that she can single-handedly control her own destiny—as her hero Benjamin Franklin appeared to do—even though she is surrounded by variables far beyond her control: "Preoccupied with her ambitions for herself and her son to escape the poverty and disillusionment of black ghetto life and wholly uncritical of the white models to which she is exposed, she has no friends or relatives with whom she seeks association, attends no church, and in her attitudes, denies the possibilities of communal sources of strength. Consequently, she was vulnerable to the greed, anger, and sexism of those who were capable of destroying her" (McKay, 135). Lutie's refusal to acknowledge "communal sources of strength" manifests itself in her self-imposed isolation. In the end, that isolation leads to her final flight into self-imposed exile. Flight, as usual, is her solution to the problem of unwanted contact. At the novel's end, however, we can predict that her departure will not solve anything.

Although her pattern of running away from relationships contributes to Lutie's downfall, it is important to remember that nobody black or white in Harlem, male or female, offers Lutie unconditional support. Because their attitudes are informed by various permutations of racism and sexism, neither her family nor her acquaintances can possibly provide Lutie with the kind of help she needs. In her encounters with these people who are just as vulnerable, angry, and fearful as she is, Lutie has little reason to think she would benefit from wholehearted participation in the community of Harlem. Contact seems to lead her inevitably *toward* danger rather than away from it. Michael Cooke identifies the paradox involved here: "[B]oth Chester Himes's *The Primitive* and Ann Petry's *The Street* leave their protagonists in grim solitude, despite powerful struggles to break into a living social pattern. Like *Native Son,* these novels involve murder, which almost comes to emblematize the ultimate ignorance of how to integrate oneself socially, even while one is experiencing ultimate physical closeness and exposure in society."[7]

In *The Street,* however, it is Boots's attempted rape of Lutie that best represents ignorance—or, perhaps more accurately, the wholesale abandonment—of acceptable socialization. By contrast, the homicide Lutie commits is the ultimate response to the sexual and racial abuse she has suffered throughout the novel. The oppression Lutie cannot escape she replicates and magnifies. Killing Boots brings her full circle from victim to perpetrator.

In her final flight from New York to Chicago (which happens to be Bigger Thomas's hometown), Lutie sees herself as a social outcast, a statistic. Not only is there no safe place left in the city for her; there appears to be no place at all for Lutie. Since the community has denied her an independent, nonsexualized identity of her own, she will continue to exist, albeit negatively, in relation to males—as a woman without a man, a mother without a son. Running away from one unhappy relationship after another, she keeps running head-on into the ways in which all of these relationships define and demoralize her. But Lutie Johnson will not be able to exist in a social vacuum; she will need a job and a home in Chicago, and both will entangle her in new relationships. If her past experience is any indication, she will never be satisfied by the desperate company that her race and gender force her to keep.

Chapter Four
Narrative Space in *Country Place*

In *Country Place* (1947) Ann Petry explores the ways in which people's relationships determine the quality of their communal life, just as her other novels and stories do. But this prompt follow-up to *The Street* has a decidedly abstract dimension to it. Although *Country Place* details the conflicts dividing classes, races, and genders, and makes use of the naturalistic techniques displayed in *The Street,* it is primarily concerned with relationships between creators and creations, real places and narrative spaces. The novel has two primary points of focus: the implicitly contentious relationship between the first-person narrator, a pharmacist called Doc Fraser, and an unnamed, omniscient narrator and the explicitly contentious relationship between Doc and his nemesis, a gossipy taxi driver known as the "Weasel." The novel's preoccupation with narrative control provides an intriguing analog to its complicated plot. *Country Place* reveals that storytelling and truth-telling go hand in hand, even when they seem to be at war.

Like Edith Wharton and Willa Cather before her, Ann Petry invokes a male narrator as a means of establishing credibility while simultaneously infusing her tale with irony. Having grown up in Old Saybrook, the small Connecticut town where her father owned the only drugstore, Petry is intimately acquainted with Doc's milieu. But since Petry is black and her white male characters are generally obtuse if not always racist and sexist, her choice of Doc Fraser as *Country Place*'s narrator is especially ironic. Educated as a pharmacist herself and employed in the family business for nearly a decade, Petry deliberately conceals in *Country Place* the autobiographical perspective informing her short stories set in and around a New England drugstore. By subjugating her black female pharmacist's identity to the persona of a white male pharmacist, Petry enacts the novel's first, and most blatant, assumption. As a novelist, she assumes the privileges— and concomitant biases—of a race and gender not her own. Doing so is an essential privilege of storytelling. Through Doc, Petry illustrates both the limits and possibilities embodied in any narrator, real or fictive.

Doc Fraser's portrayal of himself as a fair-minded storyteller ironically exposes the very blind spots he claims not to have. In the first chapter, he asserts, "I am the only druggist in the town of Lennox, and for that reason I believe I am in a better position to write the record of what took place here than almost anyone else" (4). He goes on to provide what he considers his vital statistics, because, as he says, such information "offers a clue as to how much of what a man writes is to be accepted as truth, and how much should be discarded as being the result of personal bias" (1). His repeated assurances that he is a "medium kind of man" (1) suggest that he considers himself fair and impartial—that is, the ideal medium for presenting "a true account" of the town's history (4). Yet his idea of "medium" embraces extremes: He describes himself as "medium tall, medium fat, medium old (I am sixty-five), and medium bald" (1). And, as a bachelor, he admits to "a prejudice against women—perhaps I should say a prejudice against the female of any species, human or animal" (1). He then reveals, comically, that he considers his beloved female cat to be "much closer to the primitive than a male cat" (1).

Doc does not mention his race, but we can surmise that he is white from the complete absence of racism directed his way and from his conviction that he would have married Mrs. Gramby, a wealthy white widow, had they been closer in age. By overlooking race in his self-portrait, Doc implies that his whiteness is a given. He assumes that his readers would naturally expect a white narrator. The obvious irony here is that readers for generations have expected black authors to write exclusively about black characters. By creating a white male persona, Petry challenges our own assumptions about the limits authors must impose on their creative vision.

There is much more about Doc, besides his race, that he declines to specify. Although he presents himself as honest and forthcoming, he actually tells us little about himself. We don't learn anything about his family history or his young adulthood in Lennox. We don't hear a rationale for his prejudice against women. And we never find out whether he has a specific audience in mind for his book: Is he writing solely for himself? For posterity? For a readership including or excluding his fellow townspeople?

Such questions lead us to an even more puzzling matter: What is Doc's relationship to the novel's omniscient narrator? Although Doc claims "an intimate, detailed knowledge" of his townspeople (4), an unnamed, omniscient narrator controls seventeen of the book's twenty-five chapters. This narrator knows a great deal that the pharmacist, grounded all day in his shop, could not possibly know. To give just a couple of examples, Doc could not know the intimate details of Johnnie

Roane's bedroom conversations with his wife, Glory, nor could he know either Mrs. Gramby's or Ed Barrell's last thoughts as they fall down the courthouse steps to their deaths. The chapter describing Johnnie's attack on his sexually unresponsive wife would be pure imaginative speculation on Doc's part; likewise, Mrs. Gramby's senile hallucinations and Ed Barrell's final reminiscences about sex would be beyond Doc's ken.

Even if we accept Doc's aspirations to omniscience at face value—if we believe that he knows everybody well enough to script their thoughts and private conversations—the more mundane issues of plotting still create problems. For instance, Doc would probably not have access to the note that the Weasel takes from Ed Barrell's wallet, nor would he know that the Weasel later presents the note (exposing a long-past assignation between Ed and Lil, Mearns Gramby's wife) to Mearns, who in turn presents it to his ailing mother. Suffice it to say that Doc would require a surveillance system far beyond the capabilities of a 1940s pharmacist to know all that the novel's omniscient narrator knows.

The presence of the unnamed omniscient narrator thus subverts Doc's claims to narrative control. Once we acknowledge this other narrator, whose supernatural leaps put Doc's mortal limits to shame, new questions arise: Is Doc the "real" narrator who creates an omniscient voice? Or is the omniscient narrator "real" and Doc the imagined one? How does Petry fit into this schema? Is the omniscient narrator her means of discrediting a spokesman who is white, male, and admittedly sexist? Is the omniscient voice a graphic warning, moreover, that every written account, no matter what its claims to "truth," contains a dose of fiction?

The fact that *Country Place* raises these knotty issues without resolving them suggests the book's difficult, often convoluted, nature. But its difficulties are at the crux of its meaning: In *Country Place,* narrators and characters repeatedly encircle and encroach on each other's territory. Truth seems to emerge as a by-product of the concentric circles of what is real and what is imagined. As Wallace Stevens writes in "The Noble Rider and the Sound of Words," "It is not only that the imagination adheres to reality, but, also that reality adheres to the imagination and that the interdependence is essential."[1] Petry probes this interdependence in *Country Place,* just as Stevens probes it in some of his finest poems.

The Weasel: Adversary or Accomplice?

Within the novel, Doc's stormy relationship with the Weasel embodies many of Petry's questions about narrative control. On the surface, the two characters appear quite different: Doc is a self-confident native with professional status; the Weasel is an outsider with a blue-collar job. Doc's language reflects his education; the Weasel's reflects his lack thereof. But the two men do share some traits. Both are bachelors, with time to scrutinize other people's lives. Conveniently, both have access to privileged information. The ever-attentive Weasel monitors his neighbors' comings and goings around town, while Doc keeps track of everyone's health problems and pharmaceutical needs. With their keen interest in other people, both men emerge as natural storytellers intent on squeezing a tale out of Lennox, no matter how small and seemingly bucolic a town it is.

As sneaky and malicious as his nickname suggests, the Weasel not only enjoys sniffing out trouble around town; he thrives on reporting it to Doc. Despite Doc's frequent censuring of the Weasel, we can surmise that these two have a symbiotic relationship. The scandal-hungry Weasel needs Doc to listen to his latest exposés, and Doc needs the Weasel to supply him with information he could not otherwise obtain. Because they must depend on each other for information, the upstanding Doc and the low-bred Weasel serve as each other's foils. They are competing narrators paradoxically engaged in a collaboration.

Given his crucial, yet disturbingly ambiguous, role in the narration, perhaps it is no surprise that the Weasel is the novel's most interesting character. His liabilities make him a perversely engaging figure. His real name is Tom Walker (14), but his appearance and behavior preclude anyone from addressing him by that name. He has a "sharp ferret's face" and "close-set eyes" (7). His "small hands" and "humped-over shoulders" set off his notably furtive visage (7, 16). For business attire, he wears a sweat-stained cap and keeps a cigarette tucked behind his ear (7–8). In short, the Weasel is a truly repugnant fellow.

Doc, for his part, appears fascinated by the Weasel, though he never admits as much. Because he rarely leaves his shop, Doc requires a confidant of the Weasel's mobility to move the story along. Without the Weasel, in fact, Doc would not have much of a story to tell. But the Weasel boldly exceeds the bounds of a confidant providing information necessary to advance the story's plot. The Weasel does not merely report scandal to Doc; he actively courts and creates it. Threatening to appropriate Doc's authority, he appears much closer in spirit to the novel's omniscient narrator than Doc does.

In the course of the book, the Weasel functions as an author setting up a series of crucial scenes: (1) He drives Mrs. Gramby and Mrs. Roane to Obit's Heights, where they spy Ed Barrell and Glory kissing; (2) he steals the incriminating note that Lil Gramby (Glory's mother) wrote during her affair with Ed; (3) he gives the note to Lil's husband, Mearns, who in turn gives it to his mother, shocking her nearly to death; (4) he selects Ed Barrell to help Mrs. Gramby climb the courthouse steps; and (5) he steps nimbly aside as Mrs. Gramby angrily pushes Ed away, causing both of them to tumble to their deaths. Much more than a passive witness, the Weasel orchestrates the encounters central to the novel's progression.

Setting up conflict is not the Weasel's sole intent, however. The scandals he excites provide him with wonderful fodder for his own record of Lennox. His tale-telling prowess both maddens and impresses Doc, who recognizes a rival narrator when he sees (and hears) one. Although Doc must depend on the Weasel for information, he refuses to acknowledge the extent of his dependence. When the Weasel arrives fresh from his investigative visit to Obit's Heights, Doc feigns no interest: "In doing this, I was deliberately ruining The Weasel's performance. He prefers to have your undivided attention when he talks, so that he can observe the expression on your face and thus determine whether his words are pricking the bubble of some cherished illusion of yours" (91–92). But for all of his antipathy, Doc appears intent on mastering the Weasel's storytelling technique.

Readers of *Country Place* will recognize Doc's description of the Weasel's narrative style as an accurate summary of his own methods: "He is something of a showman. He sets the stage before he tells a story, carefully identifying the characters, in order to sharpen the appetite of his listener" (92). Here we begin to see just how much Doc depends on the Weasel; it seems that he looks to the other man for style as well as content. When Doc tells a story, as the following excerpt illustrates, he also strikes the pose of a showman:

> The harsh rasp of [the Weasel's] laughter filled the store. It seemed to point up the phrases he had used as he talked: gone to the bank to count her pearls, home from the war yesterday, falling all over herself to get in his car; couldn't get a straw between them; thought their eyes would fall out on the floor of the taxi.
>
> I could fairly see Mrs. Gramby in the bank at Clinton with her safe-deposit box open in front of her. I could hear the rustle of paper as she fingered through the stocks and bonds and the old letters; could see her face light up as she gazed at a pin or a ring, reliving the past as she examined it. (94)

Rehearsing and embellishing the events in his mind, Doc tries to make the story his own. Since the Weasel has already shaped the facts into a fully formed tale, Doc can only describe the way the story comes to him: "The Weasel's words had evoked a picture of raw hurt and pain and secret, furtive love. Now he was putting a frame around it—a frame of laughter" (94–95). Significantly, the Weasel's version of the tale is not our first encounter with the events on Obit's Heights; the omniscient narrator has beaten both Doc and the Weasel to the telling of this tale. By the time Doc rehashes the Weasel's account, we are reading about the episode for the third time. The telling and retelling of the story illustrate the expanding circles of narrative that any event can generate; these circles also suggest the control that a narrator wields via the framing of events.

Doc objects more to the Weasel's "frame of laughter" than any other element of the story. In an attempt to silence his adversary, he explodes: "'For the love of God,' I said, 'can't you stop making that noise?'" (95). Although Doc dissociates himself from the Weasel's malicious reconstruction of events, he nevertheless lets us know that this version exists. His own self-righteous anger is just one more frame around the Weasel's frame. His subsequent censoring of the tale ("Don't tell anyone else what you told me" [95]) indicates his desire to control all future framings. Although he warns the Weasel that rumor mongering "will only make trouble all the way around" (95), Doc has no tangible stake in protecting the town from gossip. He has much more of a stake in acquiring the story for his own use.

Doc's furious desire to control the story is illustrated again when he realizes that he has become the Weasel's informant. Once the Weasel obtains a valuable clue from Doc's prescription record book, Doc attempts to coerce the Weasel into silence. In an ironic reference to his dual occupation as pharmacist and author, Doc declares, "I don't know what you found out in this book, but whatever it was it's none of your business" (136).

The Weasel's invasion of his narrative space so enrages Doc that he conjures up the worst punishment he can imagine: He threatens to run his rival out of town. Expulsion from Lennox would be a kind of death for both of these storytellers, since Lennox provides them with the drama and intrigue that their competing, yet ultimately complementary, narratives require. But for all of his territorial bluster, Doc cannot afford to lose his main source of information about Lennox. Although he claims to be "too old now to turn informer" (137), he nevertheless divulges the

Weasel's sordid secret, "partly as a means of relieving my conscience, and partly because it lends a further insight into The Weasel" (137). In effect, Doc settles for the best of both worlds. He enjoys the satisfactions of tattling, while protecting his informer from expulsion.

In another ironic twist, Doc's two-year-old story about the Weasel showcases the Weasel's narrative dexterity even as it exposes his immorality. Doc reveals that the Weasel courted Rosie, a mentally retarded girl who worked at a local inn. After the girl became pregnant, the Weasel "convinced her that he was Superman and that she was pregnant because of all the ice-cream sodas she had eaten" at Doc's pharmacy (142). Although Doc entreated the Weasel to marry the girl, he did not give away the Weasel's secret at the time. Hence, he considers himself "an accessory after the fact" (137), because he had erroneously assumed that Rosie would identify her baby's father.

Even though Doc is telling the story, the Weasel retains control of its outcome. The fiction that he spun for Rosie enabled him to escape community censure, and Rosie's pathetic insistence that "Superman" fathered the child ironically accords him mythic power (142). No matter that he is neither a comic-book hero nor a Nietzschean *Übermensch,* the Weasel is an ace spinner of yarns. Doc can only conclude lamely that his nemesis lacks "a conscience" (142). Such a belated, and futile, attempt to put the crafty Weasel in his place does little to secure Doc's control of the text.

The Weasel as the Town's Mirror

Determined to force every moment to its crisis, the Weasel literally drives his townspeople to despair. He is so knowing, and nosy, that he appears all-knowing. His passengers even suspect the Weasel of the omniscience that Doc spuriously claims as his own. But the Weasel does not appear to be a truly omniscient, supernatural being, since he, too, is subject to the unnamed omniscient narrator's scrutiny. In the tenth chapter, we glimpse the Weasel's private thoughts. We discover just how much the Weasel resents the class distinctions separating him from his taxi passengers:

> He wished he could see Lil's face when she heard about Glory carrying on with Ed Barrell. She would be good and mad. First chance he got he'd needle her about it. After Lil got herself married to Mearns Gramby, she began acting like she'd never known anyone as common as a taxi-driver.

But he never intended to let her forget that they were born in the same town. (105)

Even though the townspeople consider the Weasel synonymous with Lennox, he feels like a perennial outsider. But in this respect, the Weasel is more like the rest of the town than he knows. All of the other main characters, with the exception of Doc, voice feelings of disaffection and alienation from the community. A cloud of ambivalence, building toward open animosity, hangs over Lennox. The Weasel forces the other characters to confront their own hostilities even as he struggles with his own.

As an emblem of the town, the Weasel is frequently associated with mirrors. This association heightens the Weasel's intimidating aura of omniscience. During Johnnie Roane's ride home from the station, for instance, he catches the Weasel giving him "sly, sharp looks in the mirror" (16). Like Lutie Johnson recoiling from Mrs. Hedges's stare in *The Street,* Johnnie cannot "stand having [the Weasel] pry into his mind" (14). He chafes against the Weasel's "sly way of looking at you so that you weren't quite aware of it at first, but before you knew it his glance was inside you, feeling its way around" (14). It is as though Johnnie realizes he is a character in a fictive world, and he has suddenly become cognizant of his loathsome creator, a dirty-minded deity who until now has always lurked just beyond his peripheral vision. The use of the second-person extends the omniscient narrator's reach to us. The phrasing suggests that we, too, should worry about authors scripting our lives, "feeling" their way around our minds.

The Weasel's persistent staring and suggestive conversation also have sexual overtones. In a moment that recalls the scene in *The Street* where Jones rummages through Lutie's closet, Johnnie thinks that "listening to The Weasel was like having a dirty hand paw through your personal belongings, leaving them in confusion" (18). The Weasel's scrutiny is so intense that Johnnie silently declares, "I want to think. I don't want him sticking his mouth into my mind" (19). Johnnie's thoughts ironically enact the very process he finds so objectionable, since the novel's omniscient narrator is giving voice to his unspoken concerns, that is, "sticking his mouth" into Johnnie's mind.

Although one would normally look for one's own face in a mirror, the Weasel provides an alternative reflection. When Johnnie catches the Weasel's furtive glance in the mirror, he sees something of the Weasel, something of himself, something of the whole community. A brief conversation convinces Johnnie that "this little man represented [the town] and what came out of his mouth was the thinking of the town" (11). The mirror implicates Johnnie in the whole sordid enterprise. Grimly convinced that "The Weasel speaks for Lennox" (19), Johnnie admits by the chapter's end that the "rat-faced little man had managed to make him see that nothing ever was the same; nothing ever could be the same—either on the surface or deep underneath" (20). He feels just as uncomfortable about what he sees through the Weasel's eyes as he does about the Weasel's seeming ability to look inside his mind.

Glory and Mrs. Gramby likewise perceive the Weasel's alarming capacity for anticipating and shaping the events in their lives. After the infamous events on Obit's Heights, Glory worries, legitimately, that the Weasel's actions will determine her fate: "It would be The Weasel who would pass the word around. He would tell all of his passengers, out of the side of his mouth, and his eyes would watch their reaction in the mirror" (78). Glory recognizes both the Weasel's power as a storyteller and the danger that such power poses to her. She knows that much of the real damage of her indiscretion will be done in the public revelation of it. Because the Weasel serves as a conduit to the town, Glory's story will soon become many different stories in many different minds. Glory is in no position to tell her own story, so she has no authority over the form that it takes.

It is only after she decides to resurrect Johnnie's attack on her that Glory can seize control of her own narrative. In the process, she also rescripts Johnnie's story. By painting bruises on her neck, she elicits her employer's sympathy and begins the process of rehabilitating her reputation:

> She smiled at Perkins—a small smile, piteous, helpless. She could tell from the expression in his eyes exactly how right the smile was; and also from the way he blinked and swallowed. He would tell his wife that Glory was a brave little girl and that skunk Johnnie Roane had tried to kill her in a fit of rage; given to them like so many of these veterans who think they're still driving B-29's over Tokyo or something. The story would cling to Johnnie; it would crop up wherever he went; queer, not safe, not all there, Glory left him, tried to kill her, dirty skunk. (208)

Here Glory assumes the narrator's powerful role, building a new, useful story around the formerly humiliating one of Johnnie's sexual assault on her. Perhaps Glory, like Doc, has learned from the Weasel's technique. In any event, she harnesses the strength that comes not just from speaking up but from reframing events to suit her needs.

As usual, however, the Weasel arrives in time to rescript events according to his preferences. Glory expects the worst: "I don't want him staring at these bruises I painted on my neck. He's the kind would reach over and rub them to see if they would come off" (209). The Weasel actually goes Glory one better, revealing that he saw her leaving Ed's home that afternoon. The Weasel's revelation effectively ruins Glory's sympathy-inspiring account; he remains the narrator supreme. Having succeeded in trumping Glory's amateurish attempt, the Weasel heads toward Perkins, an audience already in place: "He crossed the store, heading for the counter where Perkins was. He looked back at Glory over his shoulder; his glance, sly, knowing. Then he winked" (209). The Weasel's signature gesture reveals his confidence in his ability to control any scene, any story.

Mrs. Gramby never recognizes the Weasel's adversarial qualities, but, like Johnnie Roane, she marvels over the taxi driver's ability to read her thoughts. While ruminating over the town's prejudice against Jews, she is understandably startled when the Weasel brings up that very subject: "She glanced at the back of his head, and then looked out of the car window. Mr. Weasel had an uncanny and disconcerting way of following one's train of thoughts. She had often wondered how he managed it" (87). The personification of all the town's prejudices against minority groups, the Weasel speaks for Lennox whenever he gets on the subject of Catholics or Jews. Prejudice is on everybody's mind, it seems; the Weasel, who appears capable of entering people's minds, merely brings the topic out in the open. His snickering recollections of long-standing local prejudices reflect poorly on the town. But they also reflect the Weasel's ability to keep his finger on the community's pulse, as Mrs. Gramby's thoughts acknowledge. Nobody can accuse the Weasel of not knowing his subject matter; he is a consummate storyteller with a sharp eye for the damning detail.

Moments before her death, Mrs. Gramby finally tells the Weasel what she has been thinking for a long time: "'I find you everywhere,' she said. 'Even in my thoughts. You reach them before I do'" (254). Although Mrs. Gramby has no reason to dwell on the Weasel, who functions as her lackey at large, her comments imply that he is *literally* on her mind, reading her thoughts. Echoing Johnnie Roane's thoughts about the Weasel, Mrs. Gramby anticipates postmodernist concerns with authors and their texts. Her remark suggests a character's unnervingly direct appeal to the author.

As an emblem of omniscience, the Weasel appears to be a "Superman" who knows too much for anybody's good. He sets up scenes, anticipates his townspeople's thoughts, and then shapes everything into narrative form. But as the chapter from his perspective reveals, every narrator is subject to another narrator's "framing," and every mirrored image holds the potential for a new kind of truth. Even the Weasel occasionally sees himself in the town's mirror, as the following scene indicates:

> [The Weasel] lowered the car window and spit. Wind blew the saliva back against his hand. He wiped it off on the side of his coat.
> "It's my own spit, ain't it?" he said defensively and glared at the mirror. (107)

Framed by the mirror, the Weasel addresses an image of himself as if it were a higher authority. For once, he has suffered the humiliating effects of his own crippling vision. His own spit is still spit, after all. Like Johnnie Roane, Mrs. Gramby, Glory, and Lil, he engages in a destructively self-reflexive relationship with the town. Glaring at the town's mirror ensures only that the mirror will glare back at him.

Narrators/Conspirators

After Mrs. Gramby's death, the novel ends swiftly, even abruptly. The narrative's tension is released, not by Johnnie Roane's departure or the deaths of Mrs. Gramby and Ed Barrell but by Doc's open alliance with the Weasel. The two narrators finally have the opportunity to witness important events together. Doc does not need the Weasel as a source of information, and the Weasel cannot tell Doc a story that the drama-hungry pharmacist is witnessing for himself.

In the concluding chapter, Doc and the Weasel metamorphose into conspirators. They attend the reading of Mrs. Gramby's will together and leave together. They are even accorded similar recognition: Mrs. Gramby has bequeathed the Weasel $500 for "his careful driving" and "chivalrous assistance," while Doc, "her devoted admirer," receives a diamond ring (261). Mrs. Gramby makes no significant distinction between the two men; both are relegated to the status of supplicants. But she views them in a much more flattering light than either man deserves. The Weasel's meddling has indirectly brought on her death, and Doc, having inadvertently aided and abetted the Weasel's plotting, is as much of an "accomplice after the fact" in Mrs. Gramby's death as he is in the far-from-immaculate conception of Rosie's child.

Throughout the reading of the will, Doc keeps a close eye on his adversary. His story has been filtered through the Weasel for so long that he seems incapable of seeing events without the other man's guidance. After the lawyer Rosenberg announces that Mrs. Gramby left her house to the servants, for instance, Doc immediately turns to the Weasel: "I looked at him and he was nibbling at his thumbnail, putting it in his mouth and taking it out. In his excitement, his jaws were moving just as if he were chewing food, and pausing in between to swallow" (262). The Weasel appears to be processing raw spectacle, chewing it up and converting it into narrative. Later, when the two men leave together, "The Weasel did not speak as he drove through Whippoorwill Lane, though his lips kept moving, as though he were talking to himself" (265). The town's ever-changing history serves as the Weasel's sustenance, and the events he has just witnessed have been a royal feast. The events, moreover, have presented themselves to him like a gift. Lil's explosion and Mearns's confrontation with her exceeded his own expectations of scandal. He can hardly believe his good fortune. Witnessing his townspeople in an ugly confrontation appears to be the Weasel's version of the American Dream. He does not mind saying as much: "He nudged me and whispered behind his hand, 'Hey, Doc! I wouldn't a missed this for a million dollars'" (264). We can assume that nothing would have kept Doc away, either. The reading of the will (Mrs. Gramby's attempt to rescript Lennox's history) provides him with an unusual opportunity to watch the Weasel in action.

Doc and the Weasel continue to spar lightly, even after they have joined forces as fellow witnesses and narrators. When Doc explains the meaning of "chivalrous" to the Weasel, his definition seems both ironic and indirectly self-laudatory: "Gallant. A gentleman in the old-fashioned sense of the word. Polite to old women and babies and children. Even generous to, and considerate of, other men" (266). His concluding remark—"Though I must say I fail to see how Mrs. Gramby came to that conclusion about you" (266)—would have undercut the Weasel's moment of undeserved honor, had the Weasel heard him. But the Weasel appears lost in self-satisfaction.

Gazing at his reflection in a mirror on the book's last page, the Weasel emerges finally as the ugly, and accurate, mirror into which the whole town must look. While he, too, holds illusions about himself (he is clearly not so chivalrous as Mrs. Gramby's will has for the moment convinced him that he is), he spends most of his energies destroying other people's illusions about themselves. Yet for all the trouble that he causes, the Weasel helps hold the town together at the same time that he tries to break it apart. As taxi driver, he may drive people to ruin, but he also keeps them in contact with one another and thus keeps this

depressed—and depressing—community alive. As Vernon Lattin argues
of *Country Place,*

> Johnnie is not alone in living the life of illusion and compromise; all the
> people of Lennox seem caught up in their own fantasies. Glory recreates
> herself as the heroine of movie illusion, while her mother dreams of own-
> ing the Gramby house and firing the servants who insult her. Mrs. Roane
> lives through her son's dreams; Mrs. Gramby lives the illusions of past
> glories, stifling her son's sexual and personal lives. Ed Barrell, the
> Mussolini of Lennox, deals in sexual conquest, hoping that he can thereby
> maintain an illusion of his youth (he has a bad heart) and his ego.[2]

Unified only by their selfishness and their penchant for illusion, these
characters do not appear better off after their illusions have been
exposed. Along with the town's victims of racial and religious prejudice,
they are still trapped by the community's limited mind-set. Only Neola
and the Portegee, the black housekeeper and Portuguese gardener who
inherit Mrs. Gramby's house, appear united by genuine love for each
other rather than mutual self-delusion.

Lennox as Work in Progress

Doc's preoccupation with the Weasel suggests that he is finally more interested in his fellow storyteller than in the startling events at hand. The
Weasel has become the center of Doc's story as well as its main source.
Once the Weasel bids him farewell after they return to the pharmacy, Doc
literally has nothing left to say. The book ends with the Weasel's familiar
adieu: "Don't take no wooden nickels, Doc" (266). Coming as it does at
the novel's end, the directive resonates for Doc, and for us. In his inim-
itable way, the Weasel suggests the importance of scrutinizing everything
closely, looking for fictive elements in objects that appear "real," and refusing to settle for other people's fabricated versions of truth. *Country Place*
likewise revels in the paradoxes linking tellers, tales, and interpreters.

Chapter Five

Linked Lives in *The Narrows*

Like the titles of her first two novels, the title of *The Narrows* (1953) suggests the breadth of Ann Petry's interest: the life of a whole community. *The Narrows* depicts a more malleable, diverse community, however, than either the impoverished Harlem of *The Street* or the claustrophobic little town of Lennox, Connecticut, in *Country Place.* The black characters in this novel are not uniformly poor or otherwise oppressed as they are in *The Street,* and the white characters are developed in more convincing detail than their provincial counterparts in *Country Place.* The longest and most expansive of her three novels, *The Narrows* represents the full flowering of Petry's preoccupation with human relationships. The book is as much about the connections (and disconnections) between characters as it is about the characters themselves.

All the connections take place in Monmouth, a small city in Connecticut, and the name of the city has great resonance. The novel's epigraph from *The Life of Henry V* refers to Monmouth, England, where Henry V was born: "I tell you, captain, if you look in the maps of the orld, I warrant you sall find, in the comparisons between Macedon and Monmouth, that the situations, look you, is both alike" (act 4, scene 7). The reference places Petry's Monmouth in a continuum of history and literature. Petry's story is not an analogue to Shakespeare's, yet there are points of comparison. While Shakespeare's Monmouth is the birthplace of an English king who triumphs in battle, hers is the hometown of Link Williams, a young black man who served as a Navy censor during World War II. Furthermore, while Shakespeare's play ends happily with Henry's marriage to Princess Caroline of France, Petry's novel climaxes with Link's murder, the disastrous result of his love affair with Camilla Treadway Sheffield, a white heiress (designated a princess by J. C. Powther). The allusion to *Henry V* thus creates an ironic context for Petry's story.

The content of the epigraph Petry selects is also significant. The quote is a passing reference to Monmouth by Fluellen, one of Henry's officers. Fluellen seems to consider Monmouth interchangeable with Macedon, home of Alexander the Great. In his tangential comment, he makes a valid point but misses one that is equally valid: It is true, as he observes, that on a map one town with a river may appear just like another town with another river. But it is also true that people, not just rivers, shape the character of a place. Monmouth and Macedon are distinct from each other because their people are distinct, all with ambitions and prejudices of their own. Yet each town may be a microcosm of the larger world, and it is perhaps in that paradoxical sense that Fluellen is correct: two separate communities, both microcosms, may be characterized as interchangeable.

Petry's Monmouth seems to be a microcosm of midcentury America, with the Narrows representing a microcosm all its own: a community made up almost entirely of blacks. Simultaneously part of Monmouth and a community unto itself, the black neighborhood is known to locals variously as "the Narrows, Eye of the Needle, The Bottom, Little Harlem, Dark Town, Niggertown—because Negroes had replaced those other earlier immigrants, the Irish, the Italians and the Poles" (5). In contrast to the nicknames deriding the neighborhood's racial and social status, "Eye of the Needle" ironically conflates the biblical aphorism about rich men finding it harder to enter the Kingdom of Heaven than camels attempting to pass through the eye of a needle. This nickname proves apt, since the novel ultimately reveals that rich white people cannot pass through Monmouth's black community unscathed. Furthermore, despite the negative connotations of "Niggertown" and "Dark Town," the plethora of nicknames hints at the multiple faces of a racially uniform enclave. The Narrows is far from stagnant, and its citizens, though mostly black, are quite distinct from each other.

A roll call of the Narrows' residents shows what a varied lot they are. Link Williams is a smart, flippant young man who works for the Last Chance bar. His adoptive mother, Abbie Crunch, is a puritanical widow who owns a large house on Dumble Street, the heart of the Narrows. Her friend, Frances K. Jackson, operates the local funeral parlor and employs an outspoken housekeeper, Miss Doris, and an effeminate assistant, Howard Thomas. Bill Hod, the owner of the Last Chance, is Link's hot-tempered protector and role model. Weak Knees, a war veteran subject to strange fits, is the bar's chef and Link's kind-hearted friend. Malcolm Powther, a fastidious little man who has taken rooms for his family at Abbie Crunch's home, is the butler for the Treadways, Monmouth's richest and most prominent white family. His wife, Mamie, is a large, sensual woman who is openly having an affair with Bill Hod. J.C. is the Powthers' youngest child, an unruly little boy who pesters Abbie. Peripheral characters include Cesar the Writing Man, who chalks prophetic Bible verses on the sidewalks, and the sex-starved war cripple Cat Jimmie, whose crazed pursuit of Camilla Treadway precipitates her first encounter with Link. The development of these characters—via event, dialogue, and frequent cross-reference—ensures our perception of the Narrows as a vivid, lively neighborhood.

Thus, while the central plot and the amount of text devoted to Link indicate that he is the main character, the novel is also "a saga of a community."[1] It concerns the relationships "linking" all the people in and around the Narrows, and Link himself recognizes that his life is part of a larger fabric. He considers his fate inextricably bound to the fates of Abbie, Bill Hod, and the woman he initially knows as Camilo Williams: "I have already, at the sight of that beautiful laughing face, once again, placed my trust, my belief, placed it irrevocably, in the hands of another human being. . . . First there had been Abbie Crunch, and then Bill Hod, and now—a girl" (96). Link's fate is a truly collective enterprise shaped by many people besides the principal characters he mentions. As Malcolm Powther realizes, "Link Williams had made these separate worlds coalesce, collide" (345). In the end, the ongoing life of the community subsumes Link's individual fate. When he is killed, the community as a whole must absorb and endure the loss. The residents of Monmouth must face the fact that, even in a segregated city, blacks and whites will cross paths. The fates of the races are linked, just as the lives of the people in the Narrows are.

Link's personality at age twenty-six is a work in progress. Alternately self-confident and riddled with doubt, he is consistent only in his self-consciousness. He is plagued by a heightened awareness of his past, both personal and racial, and perhaps as a result of this preoccupation with the past, he is uncertain about his identity. His uncertainties about himself immediately surface when Camilla asks about his nickname. When he explains that it is a "contraction of Lincoln" (67), the scene ripples with delayed irony, since we later learn that it is just at this moment that Camilla realizes Link is black. As she struggles to repress her fear of him and all the other black people who fill the bar where they sit, Link for the moment remains oblivious to the racially charged situation he is in. He is too busy thinking, in rather abstract terms, about racial and familial history and his place in both:

Emancipation Proclamation Williams. Named after him. Why? The women named the children, reward for services rendered, award for valor, for the act of birth, the act of creation. So the creator names the child.

What did the mother mean? What was it? Act of gratitude? A way of
saying thank you? Or perhaps some of the males in her own family had
been named Lincoln and so she, without thought, without real purpose,
simply gave the name to her male child. (67)

A history major and would-be historian of slavery, Link is at a loss when
it comes to his personal history. He appears to have no knowledge of his
biological mother. As a result, he wonders whether he was named after
Abraham Lincoln (whose history is known) or after black ancestors
(whose history is unknown). His uncertainty about his mother leaves
him uncertain about himself. Never quite sure who he is supposed to be
in regard to others, he strikes a cocky, aggressive pose to hide his self-
doubts.

The names of the other characters are as significant as "Link." The
name "Crunch" suggests a decidedly brittle character (which Abbie is),
while the name "Hod" conjures up a "hard" man (which Bill is).
"Camilo" and "Camilla" both contain a hint of "chameleon" (which
Camilla is). Camilla's chameleon quality is further underscored by her
appropriation of Link's surname, Williams, when Link asks her full
name. Attempting to blend in with the company she keeps, Camilla in
the end reveals herself to be a true Treadway, treading recklessly on others (even running over a child with her car) in the attempt to have her
own way. The names of the Powthers children, meanwhile, evoke the
Narrows' history of cultural diversity: The twins, Kelly and Shapiro,
allude to the community's past populations of Irish Catholics and Jews,
while J.C., whose initials are his name, evokes Jesus Christ. Though
hardly a Christly child, J.C. in the end appears to be the hope of
Monmouth and, as such, may yet live up to his enigmatic name.[2]

Familial Links

The relationship between Link and Abbie, one of the novel's three primary "links," helps illuminate Link's adult personality. In a flashback, we
glimpse him as an eight-year-old, worshipping the practical, seemingly
ever-reliable schoolteacher who takes him everywhere she goes: "He was
in love with Abbie in those days, he wanted to be with her all the time,
and though he called her Aunt Abbie when he spoke to her, he called her
Abbie in his mind because he thought it a beautiful name and liked to
say it" (102). In the midst of his worship, however, he notices Abbie's
class consciousness; she calls the Italian grocer by his last name,

"Davioli," and ignores Weak Knees, the Last Chance's eccentric chef (102). Her husband, the Major, takes a much more tolerant view of people. When the subject of Weak Knees and Bill Hod comes up, the Major rebukes Abbie for passing judgment on others: "Abbie, if you believe that the Lord watches over and cares about a sparrow, then you must also believe that He watches over and cares about Bill Hod" (107). The comment, Link's first indication that Abbie is not perfect, presages Abbie's flawed judgment of the Major.

Her husband's now long-ago death and the subsequent breakdown of her relationship with Link continue to trouble Abbie. Still living in the house her husband chose, across the street from Hod, who had warned her that the Major was deathly ill and then diverted Link's affections, she must confront the past every day. The memories stirred by her surroundings are as much a part of her present life as the arrival of her new tenants, Malcolm and Mamie Powther and their three rambunctious children. A passing encounter with Hod, who she now discovers is an intimate acquaintance of Mamie Powther, is enough to trigger Abbie's lingering sorrow and guilt.

The narrative's Faulknerian shifts in perspective reveal that even if Abbie is not exactly living in the past, the past is definitely living in her: "It was almost twenty years ago that it happened. All of that. Yet the sight of Bill Hod in my yard makes me keep shivering as though it were yesterday" (28). Her memories, like Link's, are woven into the novel through indirect discourse and stream of consciousness. The sections from her viewpoint reveal that Abbie has still not recovered from the traumas of two decades past. When she recalls her husband's dissolute appearance at the onset of his fatal illness, she relives feelings of humiliation rather than sympathy for her husband. She had feared that the community of Monmouth would regard her as the duped wife of a stereotypically immoral black man. Years later, Abbie knows that in fact she was duped, but only by her own unwillingness to recognize the gravity of her husband's condition.

For all of the Major's kindly traits, Abbie seems to have been profoundly uneasy around him. In the flashbacks, he is a large, rumpled, and much more relaxed person than she will ever be, and he is unabashedly proud of his ancestors and their sometimes comical exploits. He prefers the black church to the white one, and he sings in the choir, though not so often that he might be perceived as taking advantage of Abbie's role there as organist. He works, apparently without complaint, as coachman for a prominent white man. Unlike Abbie, he sees no reason to minimize his racial heritage or to censure his ancestors for their free-spirited ways. Even now, Abbie seems unable to forgive her husband for being so comfortable with himself. Her obsession with propriety suggests that she has indeed "embraced a rigid New England code of genteel behavior in order to deny her blackness and in so doing has sacrificed love" (Weir, 86).

The Major's death, followed by the temporary loss of Link, is a high price to pay for social acceptance, yet Abbie seems unwilling to change her course. Intent on assimilating into the mainstream white culture, she fails her husband and adopted son. Much of her life involves strenuous attempts "to assert equality with her white neighbors by being always more virtuous and more socially correct than they are" (McDowell, 137), but, sadly, these attempts do not always reflect as well on her as she would like.

Once Abbie realizes how ill the Major is, she reassesses her role in the crisis: "If he died it would be her fault. She should have called the doctor the moment the Major came in the house. She let him sit there. 'He's got newspapers around him.' Link's young voice. Reproach, wasn't it? The new carpet. Newspapers. The *Monmouth Chronicle.* Yesterday's. Spread out on the floor" (33). Abbie's status in the community is still foremost in her mind. She has identified her young son as a disembodied voice; his innocent observation as a reproach. By extension, the newspapers she has spread around the Major now symbolize public opinion, the forum she will be thrust into if anyone intuits her role in her husband's death. Her worst fears of exposure are validated by a message written on the sidewalk: "At her feet he bowed, he fell, he lay down: at her feet he bowed, he fell: where he bowed, there he fell down dead" (34). Cesar the Writing Man has left his mark, and Abbie infers that public, even divine, judgment has already been passed on her private tragedy.

Abbie's shortcomings as a wife and mother spring, ironically, from her desire to be a woman whose behavior is beyond reproach. Trying to be an exemplary specimen of her race, she condemns anyone, and anything, that could be construed as stereotypically "colored." She wears the plain, sensible attire of a white New England homemaker; she refuses to buy watermelons; and she recoils from the passionate emotion of the black woman singing at the Major's funeral. "At the first sound of that voice, lifted now, unearthly, terrible in its sorrow, she told herself, Think of something about him that you did not like" (35). Abbie immediately remembers the Major's elaborate stories about the high-spirited "swamp niggers" in his family (35). Even in her sorrow, anything related to black heritage or folk tradition makes Abbie extremely uncomfortable.

In her grief, Abbie allows Frances Jackson, rather than Link, to comfort her. Her old friend—whose father called her "Frank" (234)—becomes a kind of surrogate spouse for Abbie just as Bill Hod becomes a surrogate father to Link. During the ensuing years, Frances provides the tenderness and emotional strength that Abbie needs to survive. In the process, Frances also assumes importance in Link's life. She initially shields Abbie and Link from each other, causing Link at age eight to leave behind his inattentive mother for the companionship he finds in the Last Chance. Then Frances accompanies Abbie on a failed mission to bring Link back home. When Link finally returns, Frances continues to be an imposing presence in the household. An objectively reported exchange between Abbie and Link at the novel's beginning reveals their divergent views of Frances:

> "Frances didn't live here with us," she said.
>   "She might just as well have. . . . She was here so often that I used to think she was my father and you were my mother."
>   "She's been awfully good to me," Abbie said, remembering.
>   "Yeah. I don't doubt that. But F. K. Jackson is right at least ninety-nine point nine times out of a hundred. It's very difficult for us average humans to love a female with a batting average like that. If she'd been a gambler she could have made a fortune." (14)

While Abbie remembers the friendship Frances has offered her over the years, Link's teasing comments hint at smoldering resentment. He implies that Frances has habitually come between him and Abbie and that, to his way of thinking, Frances has been an oppressive influence rather than a source of comfort. By casting Frances in the role of a father, furthermore, he raises questions about her sexual preference—and Abbie's, too. (Abbie does not contradict Link's assertion about her relationship with Frances, although she seems to recognize that his comments are intended as criticism.) It seems that Abbie and Frances do not need men; they have found the companionship they need in each other, and Link cannot quite forgive either one of them for it.

In the sections of the novel told from Link's perspective, we see that his memories of the Major, Abbie, and Frances are very different from Abbie's. The Major's death leaves him in an isolated, lonely state. The security of his life with Abbie and the Major has vanished mysteriously before his eyes. In a few days, he has, in effect, lost both of his adoptive parents: "She forgot all about him. Then the Major was dead" (108). Traumatized by the sudden loss of her husband, Abbie seems incapable of being a mother, but Link is too young to be anything but a helpless, questioning son.

When he discovers Frances consoling Abbie, he thinks: "Yes, the two of them together—but what about me?" (113). It seems that Frances has usurped both his and his father's role in Abbie's life, and he never gets over his early resentment of his mother's omnipresent friend. Years later, he wonders whether Frances is a lesbian: "Perhaps she, in her own person, was the dark handsome lover, and to her Abbie had been the China Camilo Williams that the male hunts for and rarely ever finds; and even if he finds her, never quite manages to capture her" (142). Denied access to Abbie, Link can no longer sustain his childish adoration of her. His worship gives way to distrust and fear. If she refuses to acknowledge him, then he must find someone else "to put in the place that Abbie had held in his heart" (114). He must spurn the two women who have evidently spurned him.

Multiple Mothers and Fathers

Blurred gender roles form a pattern during Link's youth. Once he wanders across the street to the Last Chance—its name underscoring his desperate quest for affection—he finds a powerful father figure in Bill Hod and a motherly figure, if not exactly a mother, in Weak Knees. Thus Link leaves behind Abbie and Frances, two surrogate female parents, for two surrogate male parents. He is delighted by Weak Knees's hearty cooking and awed by Bill Hod's authority and unabashed masculinity. Bill Hod, known around town for his shady business deals, is everything Abbie despises in a black man—and Link loves him for it: "[T]his man, Bill Hod, had taken him out of the dark and put him in the sun. He had loved Abbie but in a different way, a quieter, less violent way. There was something of worship as well as passion in his feeling for Bill Hod" (119–20). The relationship between Link and Hod is the second major "link" in the novel, an exceedingly important tie that prevents Abbie and Frances from instilling only their notions of manhood and honor in their young charge.

For the rest of Link's life in the Narrows, he moves back and forth between Abbie's house and the Last Chance. Thus yoked together, his competing sets of surrogate parents share an uneasy coexistence. His male parents teach him how to cook, swim, and shoot a gun—and how to be proud of his race—whereas Abbie and Frances explain to him "the awful business of sex, and religion" (242), plan his education, and intro-

duce him to college-educated young ladies.[3] For all of their good inten-
tions, however, the adults masterminding Link's life do not provide him
with a lasting sense of security. As an adult, Link cannot forget either the
abusive treatment he suffered at Bill Hod's hands or the rejection he suffered at Abbie's.

His memories of Hod's cruelty surface during the most dramatic
moments of his adult life: after Abbie has caught him in bed with
Camilla and right before his death. In the first instance, Link must deal
with both Abbie's and Camilla's rage. Abbie has thrown him and
Camilla out of the Dumble Street house and Camilla has subsequently
called him a "black bastard" (257). Rather than think about his unstable
relationships with the two women, Link immediately thinks of Hod. He
remembers how Hod had once beaten him so badly that the doctor said,
"A man capable of doing this sort of thing to a sixteen-year-old boy
ought to be put in prison. If I were Mrs. Crunch, I would have him
arrested" (258). Throughout his life, Link feels victimized by people he
loves, and the doctor's comment makes explicit the possibility of Hod's
betrayal and Abbie's neglect. Now, Camilla's racist slur (which may contain an element of truth, since he does not seem to know the circumstances of his birth) fills Link with the kind of murderous anger that he
associates with Hod.

Since his teen years, Link has associated sexuality with violence and
shame. In a later flashback we learn the reason for Hod's assault: He did
not want Link patronizing a prostitution house that Hod himself owned.
Both times Link had gone to China's Place, China had secretly reported
his arrival to Hod. The first time, Hod had twisted Link's arm violently
and threatened to kill him if he showed up there again; the second time,
Hod had nearly kept his word. Link's worship of the older man had
begun to seem just as unfounded as his childhood devotion to Abbie.

Link cannot get Hod out of his mind even when he has more immediate crises to resolve. After Hod bails him out of jail, his thoughts again
turn to his unhappy, unsettled teenage years. He recalls, "I was going to
kill King Hod because he caught me in China's place again, and, justifiably, from his point of view, and, justifiably, according to his theory of
educating a young male, damn near beat me to death" (323). With his
flair for self-mocking irony, Link now envisions his life as a kind of
Bildungsroman or perhaps as a black man's version of *The Education of
Henry Adams:* "All part of the education of one Link Williams. A long-
drawnout affair. Can now include Camilla Treadway Sheffield as part of
the process, the finishingoff process. Can now say that I have taken the

advanced course in the graduate school" (323). Now that Camilla has
charged him with an assault he did not commit, he feels that he has once
again been betrayed by someone he loved. He responds to the disap-
pointment with his usual defense: brash cynicism.

Love, Lust, and Camilla (the Chameleon)

Although Link has ample reason to feel betrayed by Camilla, he shares
the responsibility for the breakdown in trust. Throughout their love
affair—Link's third primary "link"—he is suspicious of Camilla's motivations and refuses to take either her education (at Barnard) or her career
(as a globe-trotting fashion writer) seriously (94–95). He routinely
responds to her assertions with flip, patronizing remarks. At their first
meeting, he assumes that she is a prostitute looking for customers on the
river dock. Early in their relationship, furthermore, he tells her that she
is "much too beautiful to think" (90); he laughs at the thought of her
becoming a professor (95); and he thinks of her as "a temperamental little one" and "a rather highhanded little female" (129, 132). Perhaps
because of his difficult childhood, oscillating between Abbie and Bill
Hod, he cannot bring himself to trust anyone who reaches out to him; a
powerful self-defense mechanism takes over as soon as another person
touches his emotions.

His dismissive attitude is not limited to Camilla, however. In his
mind, women form a subspecies warranting cynical generalizations. On
his first date with Camilla, for instance, he decides that women go to
movies in search of vicarious sexual thrills: "So right after they finished
the supper dishes, they went around to the neighborhood theatre, and
sat there, legs apart, mouths open, panting a little, because now they
were young again, and there was no fat around their waists, no varicose
veins marred the flawless beauty of their legs, and the demon lover took
them in his arms" (141). As for the young black women Abbie and
Frances have been hoping he would date, "Most of them were put
together all right but they talked and talked and talked about housing
and crime, about Stalin and Churchill and Roosevelt and housing and
crime and Churchill and Roosevelt and Stalin" (62). And on the verge of
his affair with Camilla, he decides that "I'm not in love. It's
MamiePowtherChinaCamiloWilliams that has me by the throat" (126).
In short, Link does not like or respect young women very much. He
lusts after them, but quickly becomes antagonized if they turn their
attentions to the movies or attempt to talk about intellectual matters.

Callow, self-absorbed, and eager for sexual conquest, Link is ripe for a disastrous love affair.

His so-called Camilo poses just the puzzle that his restless intellect seems to crave. Her beautiful image appeals to him, yet her concealed identity (which he considers suspect long before the truth comes out) and her oppressive wealth logically preclude a lasting relationship. Given his adolescent ideas about women, a fling with an ultimately unavailable woman seems to be just about all that Link can handle at age twenty-six. Even he realizes that his marriage proposal is the impulsive act of a show-off: "He wondered afterwards why he'd asked her. Was it the absolute envy in the eyes of the news vendor, as he leaned forward, watching them?" (155). His attempts to convince himself that he was sincere seem forced: "In love with love, he thought. Was that it? No. In love with CamiloWilliamsChinaMamiePowther? No. In love with Camilo Williams" (155).

Considering that at one point Abbie had forgotten him completely, and later Hod had beaten him for visiting a brothel, perhaps Link's confused notions about women are inevitable. His relationship with Camilla seems a rebellious, necessary act, calculated to defy both Hod and Abbie. He flaunts his lovesick euphoria in front of Hod and sleeps with Camilla in Abbie's house. Despite feeling victimized by Camilla, Link clearly uses their relationship to even up old scores. It is only after the affair collapses that he begins to realize that he is still growing up, that the events in his life thus far are part of his education, not acts in a tragedy.

Link's education contains a final grim lesson, and that lesson, ironically enough, *is* tragic. When Camilla's mother and husband kidnap him and take him back to the Treadway mansion, two emotions motivate their crime: fear that a young black man may somehow have the upper hand in their lives and rage that the same man has so far escaped punishment. They do not seem to consider the possibility that Camilla may be at fault, or, if they do, they believe that eliminating Link will also eliminate the manifestation of the problem that is most reprehensible to them.

This fatal encounter finally enables Link to transcend his own feelings of fear and rage. The minutes leading up to his murder reveal that he has reached a new level of maturity. Watching Mrs. Treadway and Bunny Sheffield struggle with their emotions, he replays, one last time, his conflicts with Hod. He identifies with his captors because he understands murderous anger. But in his own case, he has long overcome the desire to kill Hod and believes with certainty that Hod and Weak Knees "had balanced the other world, the world of starched curtains and the price of butter, the world of crocheted doilies and what will people think, the world of white bedspreads and pillow shams and behavior governed by what The Race did or did not do" (405). His last thoughts, then, are as much about Hod and Abbie as about Camilla. Staring down imminent death, he is beyond outrage at Hod, Camilla, and even Camilla's mother and husband. All he wants to do is counterbalance his attackers' hatred with an irrefutable assertion of love: Three times he tells them that he and Camilla were in love. Link's life ends because they cannot tolerate such a revelation. In a city and society divided along racial lines, love between races is much like a loaded gun—threatening, potentially explosive, probably lethal. Bunny Sheffield responds to what seems to be the terrible power of interracial love the only way that he knows how, by killing Link. But Bunny cannot kill Link's "legacy" (407), the revelation that Camilla and Link were in love.

A Plethora of Smoking Guns

Although Bunny is the one who pulls the trigger, Petry makes it clear that many other people are implicated in Link's murder. Some are implicated in an obvious, circumstantial way. Powther, who suspected that his wife was having an affair with Link, had identified Link to his employers and thus enabled them to kidnap Link. Bullock, the morally compromised newspaper editor, has caved in to the demands of Mrs. Treadway, his biggest advertiser, by conducting a smear campaign in his paper against blacks. Fear motivates both men: Powther fears that he will lose Mamie to Link, and Bullock fears that if he does not acquiesce to Mrs. Treadway's demands, he will lose his business and, consequently, the luxuriant artifice of his suburban life. Powther's and Bullock's lives come in only peripheral contact with Link's, but their actions have enormous impact on his fate. They are part of a large web of deceit and betrayal, a web that makes them feel so much like victims that they finally assume the role of perpetrators.

Other peripheral characters also play insidious roles in Link's death. Cat Jimmie's crazed pursuit of Camilla—a manifestation of sexual frustration and disregard for women that is both shocking and pathetic—literally throws Link and Camilla together. The omnipresent photographer, Jubine, also contributes to Link's downfall. By photographing Camilla at her worst (in a drunken rage after a car accident) and Link at his best (in a pensive pose, like a handsome movie star), he creates indelible images that become public property. The photographs of Camilla reveal a powerful white woman's appalling loss of control and dignity, while the picture of Link shows a black man who, in the eyes of many whites, appears dangerously dignified, too much in control. These images are not the full story of Link and Camilla, but they are the story as the public knows it. In conjunction with Bullock's use of a terrifying photo of a black man (set up by the newspaper as a brutal attacker), Jubine's pictures tell just enough to stir everybody's emotions and set off multiple chain reactions of suspicion, anger, fear, and retribution.

On the homefront, J.C.'s knowledge of Link's clandestine relationship with Camilla is also a factor in Link's eventual death. J.C.'s pestering causes Abbie to throw open the door to Link's room, discover her son in bed with a white woman, and react with violent outrage. The exposure fills Camilla with shame and anger at Link. That incident is the beginning of the end of their affair; it is only a matter of time before neither Link nor Camilla can stand the pressures of race and the suspicions of betrayal bearing down on them both.

Hod and Weak Knees, for their part, supply a missing "link" in Link's knowledge of his lover. They covertly supply Link with a tabloid newspaper revealing Camilo's identity as a married heiress. It seems that his chance at happiness has been sabotaged all the way around: Abbie, Hod and Weak Knees, Malcolm Powther, and even J.C. push him toward the revelation that Camilla is an ephemeral presence in his life. She is, ironically, exactly what she seems: an impetuous young woman who is used to getting what she wants, and Link cannot bear to accommodate her any longer.

Image, memory, and entangled relationships thus create an untenable situation for the two lovers and precipitate Link's death. There is no way to separate the many strands of narrative from the complex history of Link's life, or to place the blame for his death squarely on one person. Nevertheless, Abbie tries to pin the blame on Mamie Powther, who "starts an evil action, just by her mere presence" (414). Frances Jackson blames Camilla because "She seemed to forget that she was white and Link was colored" (415). Significantly, both Abbie and Frances blame women for the tragedy of Link's death. They seem to think that Mamie and Camilla stepped outside the bounds of propriety governing female behavior; if women would only maintain the proper standard of decorum, so Abbie and Frances's thinking goes, there would be much less reason for men to enter into mortal combat with each other. Abbie goes so far as to wonder, "Why do the women always go free, as though they were guiltless?" (415). Given her own long battle with guilt and moral accountability, perhaps it is no surprise that Abbie blames women when disaster strikes; it is part of the legacy of her difficult, unresolved relationships with the Major and with Link.

For once, however, neither the guilt-ridden Abbie nor the self-confident Frances has the last word in a debate about Link. This time it is Miss Doris, Frances's cook, who hits on the truth. In a couple of blunt sentences, Miss Doris squelches the debate between Frances and Abbie. By stating that "It were everbody's fault" (415), Miss Doris puts the blame squarely on the community, not on any one individual. Miss Doris's comments suggest that the community bears responsibility for the fates of its members; coexistence breeds complicity. If Miss Doris is to be believed—and nobody in the outspoken funeral party contests her—then Link's death represents a flaw in the whole texture of the community, not just a momentary lapse in individual judgment.

A Community's Shared Blame

The sense of a community's shared blame is reminiscent of *The Street* and *Country Place.* The communities that Petry portrays in her novels are deeply troubled, and all of them are home to unhappy, often devious, people. In *The Narrows,* however, there is more hope at the book's end than at the end of her previous novels. In *The Street,* Lutie Johnson's departure from oppressive Harlem is a desperate alternative to remaining in the city and being charged with murder. In *Country Place,* the deaths of Mrs. Gramby and Ed Barrell bring about some superficial change in the town of Lennox, but no cataclysmic reordering of values. But after Link's death, there appears to be the potential for real, positive change in the Narrows. Abbie, who holds herself responsible for her husband's death and for Link's insecure childhood, makes a couple of profoundly important "links": First, she connects Howard Thomas's strange behavior with the probability that Bill Hod will attempt to harm, if not murder, Camilla Sheffield. She decides that she will try to stop Hod: "She was going to the police. She was going to tell them that she believed the girl was in danger" (427). Second, Abbie consciously connects her past life with Link, the son she has lost, and her present life with J.C., the would-be son who is always under foot. J.C. is, in effect, Abbie's "last chance."

This time, she will not turn away a little boy just because a disaster has struck her: "She heard an echo out of the past, heard Frances's voice saying, Run along now, Link, run along and play, and saw that small desolate figure leave the room, slowly, reluctantly, and tried to call him back and could not form the words" (427–28). At the end of *The Narrows,* Abbie can finally form the words needed to call J.C., to involve a child in her life rather than expel him from it.

Abbie's decisions, made in her characteristically understated fashion, suggest that Link's death is not entirely in vain. Even though Camilla is very much implicated in Link's death, Abbie resolves to protect the young woman as much as she can. In Abbie's mind, the snowballing acts of betrayal and violence have gone far enough. Abbie may eventually lose J.C. to Hod, just as she repeatedly lost Link to him, but at least she is willing to take the chance. Further, she resists the temptation to move in with Frances, who has invited her to do so. Independent to the last, Abbie is not defeated or diminished by Link's death. On the contrary, she is finally able to face the truth of her own life. Although she may not exactly transcend "the moral bankruptcy of American society and [emerge] as a spiritual victor" (Weir, 83), Abbie does take positive action that will help both Camilla and J.C. Since Mamie Powther and Hod have been having an affair for years, it is at least possible that J.C. is Hod's child. But even if this possibility occurs to Abbie, it does not prevent her from taking "this bullet-headed little boy by the hand" (428).

Margaret McDowell observes that in *The Narrows* "Petry neither pretends to provide answers to the problems she presents nor evades any of the implications of these problems" (McDowell, 135). Instead, she probes the relationships between the characters whose actions create problems. Link's death releases some of the terrible tension building up in the Narrows. He is at the vortex of the swirl of relationships that make up the novel. When he dies, Abbie Crunch, Bill Hod, and Camilla Treadway Sheffield lose their primary "link" in life, whereas other characters—Malcolm Powther, Frances Jackson, and Camilla's mother and husband, to name just a few—lose a secondary "link" of crucial importance to their interaction with others. For Malcolm Powther, Link was a threat to his marriage to Mamie; for Frances Jackson, Link was a basis for her friendship with Abbie but also a bothersome intrusion on it; and for Mrs. Treadway and Bunny Sheffield, Link was the object of all the frustration, fear, and anger aroused in them by Camilla's decision to have an adulterous affair with a black man.

Link, then, is an emblem of all the thought and emotion that people invest in their relationships with others. His race, gender, and age evoke categorical reactions in *Chronicle* readers, while both Jubine and Bullock see Link as an icon of black maleness, an icon whose meaning will depend on the person beholding his image. Abbie and Hod see him as a son, while Camilla sees him alternately as lover, beloved, and traitor to her affections.

Many things to many people, Link dies on the brink of the self-knowledge that he has been seeking his entire life. Having ended his affair with Camilla and apparently come to terms with Bill Hod, he is in an ideal position to fulfill his dreams and become a scholar of African-American history. But instead of becoming a recorder of that history, he becomes an entry in it. After his death, his fellow blacks in the Narrows must resume their slow progress toward equality. Neither demon nor Christ figure, he leaves them behind in a flawed but not entirely hopeless world.

When Abbie reads the local paper after Link's death, realizing that Bunny Sheffield and Mrs. Treadway have been ruined, no matter how light the sentence the court metes out, it is clear that the novel is not simply a cautionary tale about white people victimizing blacks. The pervasive impression left by *The Narrows* is of a community in flux. Reasoning seems just as likely as riot; growth, as likely as decay.

Abbie, the former teacher, learns a valuable lesson from Link's death. For the first time in her life, she is willing to accommodate people who do not meet her exacting standards: a little boy whose actions led to her horrified discovery of Link and Camilla, and Camilla herself, whose actions led to Link's death. For a woman generally so rigid in her behavior, Abbie's generosity of spirit is an astonishing about-face, a possible harbinger of good things to come for the Narrows. But the fact remains that Monmouth as a whole remains a city more racially divided than ever, and the Treadway munitions plant, with all of its connotations of violent, destructive power, is the city's economic mainstay. Abbie alone will be unable to solve all the social ills afflicting Monmouth. Now that World War II is over, the city need not revolve forever around the manufacture of guns and other weapons, nor must it be constricted by racial antagonism. Abbie Crunch is not the only person who can seize a last chance and find new, more positive, links within her community.

Chapter Six

The Wheeling Stories:
Prejudice as a Matter of Perspective

In *Miss Muriel and Other Stories* (1971), Ann Petry reveals her continuing fascination with the way people are shaped by the company they keep. Although these stories were originally published over a long period of time, from the 1940s to 1971, they cohere geographically and thematically. All of the works take place in New York or New England, and, while taking up a multiplicity of perspectives, they share a preoccupation with race, gender, and class, among other characteristics that often incite prejudice. But Petry's stories, like her novels, refuse to settle for easy truths. They do not moralize, and they do not avoid showing minority characters who inflict pain as well as suffer from it. For Petry, prejudice in all its permutations is finally a creative force. In *Miss Muriel,* individuals, their relationships with others, and their communities are clearly formed by human bias, not just harmed by it.

Five of the collection's thirteen stories are set in the fictional village of Wheeling, New York. The Wheeling stories draw on Petry's experience growing up and living as an adult in the small town of Old Saybrook, Connecticut. There is a great deal of realistic description of Wheeling's shops, streets, and geographic location, and the family that appears in three of the stories has much in common with Petry's own. The stories, like the town they portray, are multifaceted and defy easy categorization.

The book begins with a series of four Wheeling stories: "Miss Muriel," "The New Mirror," "Has Anybody Seen Miss Dora Dean?," and "The Migraine Workers." The collection's ninth story, "The Witness," returns to Wheeling. When read in sequence, these stories gradually move forward in time. The first two take place in the early twentieth century, the third moves back and forth from midcentury to the narrator's childhood, the fourth takes place in the late 1960s, and "The Witness" reflects the social environment of the late 1960s or early 1970s.

In addition to the time, the narrative point of view in these stories also shifts. The narrator of the first three Wheeling stories appears to be the same character at different points in her life. Although she is never identified by name, her circumstances as a black female whose parents run a drugstore remain constant. In "Miss Muriel" she is twelve years old; in "The New Mirror" she is fifteen; and in "Has Anybody Seen Miss Dora Dean?" she is forty-two, recollecting events that occurred when she was nine. "The Migraine Workers," however, is written in the third-person from the perspective of a Hispanic man who runs a truckstop, and "The Witness," also in the third-person, takes up the experience of a sixty-five-year-old black man. Reading the stories in order, we can see how Petry's portrayal of Wheeling changes with the times. Whereas "Miss Muriel," "The New Mirror," "Has Anybody Seen Miss Dora Dean?," and "The Migraine Workers" all delineate significant conflicts within the community, they also have a gently humorous quality about them. That quality vanishes altogether in "The Witness," a violent story pitting the town's corrupt white teenage boys against a black high school teacher.

"Miss Muriel": Prejudices in the Eye of the Beholder

The fifty-seven-page title story, drawing on Petry's childhood as the daughter of a New England pharmacist, introduces the collection's wide-angle focus on prejudice. Although "Miss Muriel" is concerned with prejudice in a small community, it is not limited to one particular strand of human bias. Instead, the story illustrates how numerous prejudices—of race, gender, sexual orientation, and age, to name a few—coexist and paradoxically create the very community that they threaten to destroy.

For the narrator of this complicated tale, Petry makes a seemingly ingenuous selection: a twelve-year-old girl. Like Petry, the narrator grows up in the early twentieth century, the daughter of middle-class African-American parents. Her family lives in Wheeling, New York, a small town similar to Petry's native Old Saybrook. Also like Petry, the narrator spends much of her time in the family pharmacy where she hears conversations that fuel her imagination and influence her notions of adulthood. And, like the future author of *The Street* and *The Narrows*, this character is acutely aware of people's attitudes toward one another. By adopting the perspective of a girl, however, Petry does more than draw on her own background and personality. She also succeeds in defamiliarizing adult biases and assumptions. Through the eyes of a twelve year old, adults appear newly enigmatic, comical, evasive, defensive, and flawed. We begin to see that their (or, more precisely, our) assumptions about each other do not have fixed boundaries; prejudice is rarely a clear-cut matter of sexism, racism, or any other "ism."

Although "Miss Muriel" is never explicitly identified as a diary (a conventional genre for a young writer), the story takes that form in its loosely episodic, ostensibly artless progression. Like a diarist, the narrator records events shortly after they happen. This format gives the story a compelling immediacy and accommodates the speaker's struggle to understand the nuances of her story. When her young, beautiful aunt (who lives with the family) becomes the object of male attention, the narrator can neither forestall nor fully comprehend the conflicts at work within her community, her family, and herself. She can almost (but not quite) see the convoluted interactions among her family members and acquaintances as a forewarning of what her own future holds.

On the verge of adolescence, the narrator is understandably fascinated by her aunt's love life. She takes an active interest in Sophronia's three suitors, Mr. Bemish, Chink Johnson, and Dottle Smith. Her detailed descriptions reveal that each man believes that he has the right to invade the family's pharmacy/home and pursue Sophronia on her turf. Although the three are very different from one another, they share the assumption that Sophronia is a pretty object rather than a person in her own right. Their rivalry shows how courtship can evolve into a conflict in which the pursued woman has no voice or power.

The suitors are themselves objects of prejudice, however. We learn from the narrator that the shoemaker, Mr. Bemish, has at least two obvious strikes against him: his age and race. His glass eye makes her feel "squeamish" (2), and the rhyme with Bemish sets the stage for an unsettling portrait of a distinctly undignified old white man. The second suitor, Chink Johnson, is a tall, swaggering black man whose appearance and undocumented past call his integrity into question. The opposite of the simpering Bemish, Chink is a blues pianist who has recently found work at the Wheeling Inn. Chink laughs harshly, dresses rakishly, and affects a scruffy beard. The name "Chink" sounds hard and tough (far from the soft, yielding sound of "Bemish"), reflecting his aggressive demeanor. Possibly a nickname, "Chink" is also an ethnic slur, an indication that Chink Johnson is considered an outsider even among fellow blacks. Sophronia's third suitor, Dottle Smith, appears to be parodying the other men's behavior rather than truly courting Sophronia. His apparent homosexuality is the main strike against him. An old friend of the narrator's uncle, Dottle is a large, light-skinned man with a penchant for reciting poetry. Dottle's ambiguous, plump-sounding name is open to interpretation, as are his swaying walk and theatrical mannerisms.

In addition to scrutinizing her aunt's suitors, the narrator ponders her father's reactions to the three men. Because he finds all of them objectionable, the narrator must struggle to distinguish her reactions from his. Her father is prejudiced against Bemish's race and age, Chink's sexually suggestive music and lower-class status, and Dottle's homosexuality. The range and vehemence of his objections imply that he might well censure anyone interested in his sister-in-law. Although Sophronia is an adult capable of making her own choices, he is extremely protective of her.

He explains his furious reactions by telling Sophronia, "It's just that we're the only black people living in this little bit of town and there aren't any fine young black men around, only this tramp piano player, and every time I look at him I can hear him playing some rags and see a whole line of big-bosomed women done up in sequined dresses standin' over him, moanin' about wantin' somebody to turn their dampers down" (48). Clearly, he feels threatened by Sophronia's suitors, especially the virile Chink.

As the narrator observes early on, neither her father nor Sophronia can bear to mention Chink Johnson at the dinner table: "Perhaps they are afraid he will become a part of the family circle if they mention him" (27). The father does everything he can to keep his family's private life separate from the public life of the pharmacy. The suitors' invasion of his family's personal space angers him, and that anger in turn creates tension in the household.

Like the suitors, the narrator's father believes that he has the right to control Sophronia's destiny. He in effect enters into the rivalry with them. Moreover, his patriarchal interest in Sophronia's love life casts his college-educated sister-in-law in the role of a child, not much different from the narrator. Significantly, it is the narrator's mother, not Sophronia, who reprimands the father for interfering. Sophronia herself does not assert her right to run her own life.

The narrator's opinions of the suitors are just as subjective as her father's. Although she identifies all three as her friends, her views are influenced by her father's negative reactions and her own emerging prejudices. Even as she proclaims her friendship, her contact with the three men reveals strong feelings of ambivalence. In regard to Mr. Bemish, for example, she must confront both her own and his prejudices about age. Convinced that he is condescending to her because she is a child, she chastises the old man for calling her "girlie" instead of addressing her by name (3).[1] Then, when Bemish claims he is too old to remember all the neighborhood children's names, she asks him with deadpan impudence: "Does the past seem more real to you than the present?" (3). Although she is many years his junior, the narrator treats Mr. Bemish as her equal or sometimes even as her inferior. This appropriation of authority is startling, especially considering the era in which the story is set: Children in the 1920s were not encouraged to speak so glibly to their elders.

Bemish's behavior, however, does not exactly inspire respect. He is an unimposing man who bakes cookies and keeps a cat named May-a-ling, and his undignified pursuit of Sophronia contains a distinct element of slapstick. In one doomed attempt to impress his beloved, he shows up at the pharmacy in formal attire and clicks his heels in the air. The narrator looks on in bemused fascination. Even at the end of the story, when she realizes that Mr. Bemish desperately needs an ally—and she tells Chink and Dottle, "He's just a little old man and he's my friend and I'm going to help him" (55)—her attitude toward him remains a mixture of sympathy, superiority, and cool-headed curiosity. Although she tries to reassure him that Chink and Dottle would not "sew" him up with his own thread, as they have threatened to do, she also pumps him for more information and wonders, "Sew up? Sew up what—eyes, nostrils, mouth, ears, rectum?" (56). This eccentric figure's imminent departure will deprive her of a source of endless fascination and diminish, if only by one person, her contact with the community of Wheeling.

The narrator's relationship with Chink is equally complicated. His presence is far more powerful than Bemish's, so she cannot pull rank on him. Her relationship with him raises the issues of sexuality and male dominance. Chink's sexuality is as intimidating as it is intriguing. At twelve, the narrator cannot ignore either his virility or his disturbingly sensual music. His overt masculinity provides a bracing contrast with Bemish's asexual foolishness and Dottle Smith's homosexuality. The narrator seems to take a voyeuristic pleasure in Chink's increasingly successful courtship of Sophronia: "Almost every afternoon he goes for a walk with Aunt Sophronia. I watch them when they leave the store. He walks so close to her that he seems to surround her, and he has his head bent so that his face is close to hers. Once I met them strolling up Petticoat Lane, his dark face so close to hers that his goat's beard was touching her smooth brown cheek" (37–38).

Interestingly, this passage follows the narrator's encounter with Chink. Having failed to win the upper hand in conversation with him, the narrator suffers an angry rebuke from Chink and bursts into tears. He responds by kissing her cheek and explaining his anger. Rather than dwelling on her humiliation, the narrator notes that Chink "smelled like the pine woods, and I could see pine needles in his hair and in his beard, and I wondered if he and Aunt Sophronia had been in the woods" (37). No longer just a spectator, the narrator intuitively connects her experience with her aunt's. Like Sophronia, she seems to consider Chink the most viable of the three suitors.

Yet the narrator does not trust Chink. She decides that he "is not a gentleman" (27), and Chink's behavior seems to bear out that class distinction. As she and Sophronia watch in dismay one afternoon, Chink drives a wagon full of giddy young women into the woods, with one woman perched flirtatiously on his lap. He is "singing a ribald song" (43), the narrator notes. The virility that has beguiled both aunt and niece evidently has just as powerful an effect on other women, and Chink plays it for all it is worth. Although his race and class may have prevented him from achieving a high social status, his sex enables him to wield power over others. He does not hesitate to assert that power, regardless of how his behavior may be interpreted by Sophronia, the main object of his desire.

The narrator's relationship with Dottle Smith is influenced by both her familiarity with him and her conviction that he is not romantically interested in her aunt. She is delighted that he is visiting her family again, as he does every summer, but she is aware of his sexual difference: "I wondered if Dottle had come alone this time or if he had a friend with him. Sometimes he brings a young man with him. These young men look very much alike—they are always slender, rather shy, have big dark eyes and very smooth skin just about the color of bamboo" (31). She knows that Uncle Johno's wife routinely leaves town when Dottle shows up, and her father is emphatic in his disapproval of Dottle, whom he denounces as "that poet or whatever he is, all he needs are some starched petticoats and a bonnet and he'd make a woman" (47). Knowing that Dottle is homosexual, even though she does not use that knowledge against him, inevitably complicates the narrator's view of her old friend.

At twelve, the narrator is becoming more perceptive about issues of sexuality. She is convinced that Dottle's elaborate attentions to Sophronia are a charade, a matter of going "through the motions" (40). In his self-appointed role as comically attentive beau, Dottle is mocking both Chink and Mr. Bemish. And in making fun of the other men, he is also making fun of Sophronia. She is a pawn in his game, a means by which he parodies two heterosexual men. Although the narrator does not come to such explicit conclusions, she is able to distance herself sufficiently from Dottle to describe his maneuvers in detail. His arch behavior in the company of Sophronia and the other suitors stands in stark contrast to his kindly treatment of the young narrator. In the company of a child, he is a pleasant, high-spirited companion who does not feel the need to flaunt his sexuality or parody heterosexuals. But among adults, Dottle reverts to type: He is an outsider at odds with the mainstream society, and the artificiality of his behavior does not escape the narrator's scrutiny.

The narrator's relationship with Dottle is further complicated by his racial militancy. She observes that Dottle and her Uncle Johno are "what my father calls race-conscious" (31). Although both Dottle and Johno are light enough to pass as whites, they adamantly insist on their minority racial status. Dottle's stories and jokes reveal his preoccupation with race, and the narrator, struggling to understand her objections to Mr. Bemish's color, admits, "I believe that my attitude towards Mr. Bemish stems from Dottle Smith" (31). She is not convinced that race alone is a sound basis for determining allies and enemies. The story's opening scene, in which she cheerfully describes her best friend, a white girl with whom she has much in common, indicates her relative freedom from racial prejudice. But from her observations of Dottle and Chink, she learns that race is of vast importance to adults—and that race relations are hopelessly entangled with relations between the sexes.

The narrator's race consciousness receives a jolt when she gets caught in the middle of the adults' ever-smoldering, if never fully articulated, dialogue about race and sexuality. The trouble starts when she parrots one of Dottle's race-related jokes to Chink. Chink is not amused by the narrator's temerity or the joke's punchline—a white clerk insisting that a black customer ask for "Miss" Muriel cigars. Refusing to accept humor at a black man's expense, Chink brusquely tells the narrator, "It ought to be the other way around. A black man should be tellin' a white man, 'White man, you see this picture of this beautiful black woman? White man, you say *Miss* Muriel!'" (37).

Regardless of the race of the man delivering the inane put-down, the joke has a sexually charged subtext. "Muriel" is portrayed as an object, not a person, whose ownership will be decided by men. The bickering over courtesy titles—the crux of the joke—alludes to large issues of race relations and sexual politics. These are public issues that nevertheless determine the quality of personal relationships.

The dispute over the cardboard "Muriel" is analogous, in fact, to Sophronia's situation. Routinely perceived as an object by her suitors,

Sophronia is the story's least expressive character. Her would-be boyfriends pay scant attention to her infrequently expressed wishes as they battle among themselves. Like "Muriel," she is a possession whose ownership is up for grabs. Despite the advantages of her education and professional status in the community, Sophronia plays a poignantly passive role in the drama of her own life.

At the story's conclusion, Sophronia's suitors are put to a small but significant test of character. When a flock of bats suddenly enters the pharmacy, Dottle Smith flees the room, Chink Johnson strikes out at the bats violently but ineffectually, and Mr. Bemish embraces Sophronia and publicly declares his love for her. The arrival of the narrator's father, who has sense enough to shoo the bats outside, ends the battle but not the war. Bemish's apparent success with Sophronia subsequently causes Chink and Dottle to join forces against the frail old man and drive him away from town. Different as the two black men are, they are allied in their opposition to Bemish. Sophronia is a black woman, and they will not let a member of the "enemy" race consort with her any longer. For Dottle, the violent act is primarily a matter of racial prejudice, while, for Chink, it is one of both racial prejudice and sexual dominance.

Chink and Dottle essentially act out the "Miss Muriel" joke as Chink prefers it: They deny a white man access to a black woman, whom they claim as their property. The story ends abruptly with the narrator's angry reaction to their vigilante justice: "You both stink. You stink like dead bats. You and your goddamn Miss Muriel—" (57). She is no longer a child on the sidelines but a disillusioned young adult witnessing prejudice, both racial and sexual, in action. Her use of invective suggests not only her anger and frustration but also her emancipation from childhood. By passing judgment on Chink and Dottle, however, she implicates herself: Now she, too, is caught up in the morass of prejudiced adult relationships.

Bemish's expulsion means one less rival for Sophronia's hand, but his departure hardly solves the social problems deeply embedded in this small community and, by extension, the whole society. Prejudices based on race, gender, sexual preference, and age will continue to flourish in Wheeling, since all of the remaining characters seem to have at least one damning strike against them. There is no guarantee of social acceptance for anyone, not even the narrator, who seems so confident at the story's beginning. They are all at risk, all potential objects of expulsion, like Mr. Bemish.

But "Miss Muriel" does not condemn Wheeling for its residents' narrow-minded views. Instead, the story shows that one form of prejudice rarely exists in isolation from other forms. The identity of Wheeling stems from its complex mix of prejudices rather than the citizens' stand on a single issue of race, gender, sexuality, or age. The tensions between men and women, young and old, insiders and outsiders keep the people of Wheeling engaged in an endless debate. In its meandering, deceptively naive way, "Miss Muriel" illustrates the ways in which prejudice, no matter how destructive a force it is, also creates the social environment in which people live and die.

Painful Reflections in "The New Mirror"

"Miss Muriel" is the first of Petry's three stories written from the youthful perspective of the pharmacist's daughter. The volume's second and third stories—"The New Mirror" and "Has Anybody Seen Miss Dora Dean?"—also deal with the narrator's changing perceptions of adult prejudices.

In "The New Mirror" there is no longer the pretense that the narrator is writing down episodes right after they take place. She is fifteen years old now, and she is much more aware of her role in the life of her family and her town. She is also becoming more self-aware. When she looks in her family's new bathroom mirror, she scrutinizes her appearance, as teenagers always do, and recoils from her dark-skinned image. As the story's title suggests, she is beginning to perceive herself and her family members as they believe the nearly all-white community perceives them.

The disappearance of Samuel Layen is the story's catalyst. On the beautiful May morning when the story begins, he is at home with his wife and daughter, talking happily at the breakfast table. By noon, he is inexplicably missing, and his absence throws the family into a panic. His wife and sister-in-law expect that the town of Wheeling will view a missing black man with suspicion rather than concern, and his daughter quickly absorbs their acute anxiety. Her mind filled with macabre possibilities, she suddenly sees her father in a new light: "I practiced different versions of the story. 'Young woman finds short, thick-bodied, unidentified black man.' 'School children find colored druggist in river.' 'Negro pharmacist lost in mountains.' 'Black man shot by white man in love duel.' Colored druggist. Negro pharmacist. Black man. My father?" (78).

Once he has vanished, it seems that Samuel Layen's private identity has vanished as well. Underscoring the importance of the "family circle" introduced in "Miss Muriel," the narrator had earlier "relished the thought that the steady stream of white customers who went in and out of our drugstore did not know what our dining room was like, did not even know if we had one. It was like having a concealed weapon to use against your enemy" (62). But Samuel's disappearance effectively disarms the narrator as well as her mother and aunt. None of them can stave off the public's interpretation of their private tragedy. Although they may possess a physical space where the white members of Wheeling cannot intrude, they remain vulnerable mentally and emotionally to the rest of their town. Their fears are so internalized that they do not need actual contact with whites to feel threatened. Convinced that exposure will precipitate censure, they are undone merely by their fatalistic anticipation of disapproval.

In addition to highlighting the family's vulnerability to the community, Samuel Layen's disappearance also gives the narrator a new perspective on her family's relationships. She realizes for the first time how much her seemingly self-sufficient mother and aunt depend on Samuel to hold their lives together. Her usually quiet, controlled aunt jumps to horrific conclusions about Samuel's absence, weeping openly and speculating out loud that he must be dead or in grave danger. Her mother, though resisting the temptation to cry, speaks in an unusually loud, harsh voice. In Samuel's absence, both women quickly lose their bearings. The narrator realizes that her father has served as the family's first—and apparently only—line of defense against danger. Without a man to protect them from the outside world, her mother and aunt seem to shrivel up: "They looked like little old women—humble, questing, moving slowly. When they turned, I could see the white part of their eyes under the irises, and I had to look away from them" (79–80).

Appalled by their seemingly spontaneous diminution, the narrator no longer sees her mother and aunt as sources of strength but rather as emblems of defeat and despair. Like the newspaper accounts of her father's death that she imagines, the two women metamorphose into vulnerable objects of public scrutiny. The narrator's ability to see them in this new light indicates that the public—or "white"—way of viewing black people has become part of her consciousness. This Du Boisian double consciousness suggests that she has forever left behind the innocent pleasures of the private, tree-filled backyard. Her fall from grace, like Adam and Eve's, involves the shame of self-knowledge.

Samuel's eventual return only sharpens the pain of her acute awareness. Wearing his newly acquired false teeth, he explains to his daughter that he had looked at himself in the new mirror that morning and decided that, as a choir soloist, he could no longer subject the church congregation to his toothless mouth. Given that in this nearly all-white town the church members would also be primarily white, Samuel's decision appears to be a concession to whites' expectations. But his dentures are more of a burden than a blessing; he looks as uncomfortable as he says that he feels. And his action is a burden on the narrator, too, since she had frequently hinted that he should buy dentures.

Her father's reappearance provokes a new set of disturbing revelations: The narrator realizes that her beloved father has been caught between one racist image of a black man with "white teeth flashing in a black and grinning face" and an equally degrading image of the "toothless old Uncle Tom" (87). With or without teeth, Samuel Layen cannot escape stereotyping: "So he was damned either way. Was he not? And so was I" (87). It seems that there is no right way for her or her family to act or react. No matter how intelligent or law-abiding they are, they will always be seen in the distorting mirror of prejudice that is as much a part of their own vision as society's.

In the end, the narrator joins in the collusion that she now considers necessary to preserve her family's privacy: She calls the police station and announces that her father has found his missing watch. It is a small lie with large meaning. Like her Uncle Johno and Dottle Smith in "Miss Muriel," she is now "race-conscious"—that is, fully aware of her distrust of white people. Although no one in her family has committed a crime, she assumes that she must lie to the white police officer to protect her family's reputation. Like her parents, she now thinks about the image she projects to the white community as well as about the truth of her own experience. She has internalized both her mother's horror of exciting public scrutiny and her father's desire to put on the face most acceptable to the public. The prospect of embarrassment pales in comparison to her new conviction that her family must lie to be accepted.

Narrative Bias in "Has Anybody Seen Miss Dora Dean?"

In keeping with the Wheeling stories' overarching theme, "Has Anybody Seen Miss Dora Dean?" looks at the way prejudice determines people's estimations of one another. But unlike the others, this story is particularly concerned with the creative prejudice of the storyteller. Its juxtaposition of memory and present-day events results in an elaborately layered fiction that invokes, in an understated way, the narrative techniques of modernist authors such as William Faulkner, James Joyce, and Virginia Woolf. Like *Country Place,* "Has Anybody Seen Miss Dora Dean?" is just as concerned with the relationships between narrators and subjects—the whole process of tale-telling—as it is with the tale that it tells.

The forty-two-year-old narrator is a much older, more mature version of the girl narrating "Miss Muriel" and "The New Mirror." Yet her recollections hark back to her childhood. Having been summoned to the deathbed of Sarah Forbes, an elderly friend of her mother's, the adult narrator recalls events and conversations dating back to the year she was nine. The story thus returns to the drugstore setting and the Layen family, comfortingly familiar to readers of the first two Wheeling stories. "Has Anybody Seen Miss Dora Dean?" is far from comforting, however. It is the most subtle of the three drugstore stories, and its movement back and forth from present to long-ago past gives it an unsettling ambiguity.

The story's seemingly whimsical title refers to a turn-of-the-century ragtime song that John Forbes, an effete butler and family acquaintance, would whistle as he bicycled around Wheeling. The narrator admits that it was years before she understood the song's effect on her father: "I suppose it amused my father to think that Forbes, who seemed to have silver polish in his veins instead of good red blood, should be whistling a tune that suggested cakewalks, beautiful brown girls, and ragtime" (96). Forbes, in fact, evokes many emotions in the family besides amusement. After he commits suicide when the narrator is nine, his life story immediately becomes part of her family's lore. The narrator's parents cannot solve the riddle of his death, nor can they put it out of their minds.

As a child, the narrator tries to piece together a life for Forbes, an enigma whom she never actually met. She draws on the conversations she overhears, the pictures in her mother's scrapbook, and her imagination to flesh out a story for him. Everything she learns interests her: She is bemused by his late, unlikely marriage to Sarah Trumbull, an outgoing, pretty girl much like the title character in the song "Has Anybody Seen Miss Dora Dean?" She is fascinated by the mysterious synergism between Forbes and Mrs. Wingate, his wealthy (and grotesquely fat) white employer. And she is obsessed with his suicide, which she mentally transforms into a play. In her child's mind, "The train whistles, and Forbes walks up the embankment and lies down across the tracks. The train comes roaring into sight and it slices him in two—quickly, neatly. And the curtain comes down as a telephone rings in a drugstore miles away" (102). As strange and oblique as a Beckett play, the drama the girl reenacts throughout her childhood reveals the creative potential that Forbes's life holds for her.

At forty-two, the narrator sees new complexities in the tale. She acknowledges that she grew up hearing Forbes's story endlessly rehashed, even though he was not a close family friend. Since she never met him, what she knew or imagined about him was based solely on her parents' recollections and impressions. It seems that his appalling death was "a theatrical reality" for her parents as well as for her (101). Although Forbes and his wife, Sarah, had niches in society (Forbes as a beloved servant and Sarah, after her husband's death, as a shrewd landlady), the narrator's parents viewed them as anomalous, troubling figures. The narrator recalls: "The conversations in which my parents conjectured why Forbes killed himself were inconclusive and repetitive" (100). Ironically, her mother blames the suicide on Sarah's poor housekeeping, whereas her father blames it on Forbes's ambiguous sexuality. He suggests that Forbes was "so ladylike" that an extramarital affair with Mrs. Wingate, his wealthy white employer, was unlikely (100), yet he also wonders why Forbes killed himself in an area filled with brothels: "It seems like a strange part of the city for a respectable married man like Forbes to have been visiting" (101). Each blaming the spouse with whom they could identify more readily, the narrator's parents betray at least a hint of anxiety about their own marriage. By taking sides as they do, they demonstrate to each other (and to their eavesdropping daughter) an awareness of the ways in which husbands and wives fail each other. Furthermore, they intimate, by their censorious views of Sarah and Forbes, that they will not make the same errors that they assume the other couple made.

The suicide that fascinates the family so much has a racial dimension as well as a domestic one. The narrator believes that her family saw Forbes's suicide as a damning commentary on being black. This is a matter of narrative interpretation, however, since the family has not read Forbes's suicide note to Sarah, and the narrator has not heard her parents explicitly connect Forbes's death with his race. But Forbes's act flies in the face of the African-American preoccupation with survival. A rather innocuous man whose brief foray into turn-of-the-century urban nightlife is mildly comical, if not completely out of character, Forbes has left behind a difficult legacy regarding the status of black people. As the narrator describes her family's reaction: "His death seemed to have put them on the defensive. They sounded as though he had said to them, 'This life all of us black folk lead is valueless; it is disgusting, it is cheap, it is contemptible, and I am throwing it away, so that everyone will know exactly what I think of it'" (94). By choosing sudden death over the drawn-out complexities of survival in a racist society, Forbes has left other blacks to question the value of their lives. Implicit in the narrator's family life is the assumption that their struggle to contribute to the community is worth the effort, despite the potential for humiliation. Forbes's suicide casts a long shadow over that assumption, since he has made it quite clear that he, for one, does not care to struggle any longer.

The questions that Forbes's death raises remain unanswered decades later when the narrator arrives at Sarah Forbes's Bridgeport home. Slipping in and out of consciousness, Sarah holds court, directing her son Peter and grandson Lud to do her bidding. The narrator discovers that Sarah also intends to leave a legacy, though a very different one from her husband. When the narrator protests that Sarah's grandsons should inherit the antique cups Sarah is giving to her, the dying woman seizes the opportunity to tell her side of the long-ago story. By way of explaining why her grandsons are not worthy of the gift, Sarah declares that they "will run with whores," just like their father and "[j]ust like Forbes tried to do, only he couldn't" (110). In her version of the story within a story, Forbes's impotence caused him to commit suicide, and his death was part of the larger tragedy of *her* life: "'I cried for three days afterward. For three whole days.' She paused again. 'I wasn't crying because of what happened to him. I was crying because of what had happened to me. To my whole life. My whole life'" (110). The repetition effectively underscores Sarah's point of view.

Although the narrator does not comment on Sarah's startling revelations, evidently Sarah (who dies shortly after the narrator leaves) feels that she has provided the missing piece to the puzzle of Forbes's death. In reality, Sarah's explanation makes the whole tale even more complex. Whereas the narrator and her family had seen Sarah as a secondary figure in a drama starring Forbes, Sarah sees her late husband as a supporting player in the story of her own long, unhappy life. Just as she wants to bequeath the valuable cups to someone who will value them, she also wants to bequeath her version of the family story to a storyteller who will preserve the narrative for future generations.

The dusty cups, with their understated beauty, become a symbol of the half-known, half-imagined past. As she cleans them, the narrator decides that they "could easily have belonged to one of the kings of France" (111). As suggestive as she is observant, she examines the cups carefully and records what she knows of their origin and design. It is no accident that she is scrutinizing the cups, and imagining their history, when the call comes informing her of Sarah's death. As the narrator first of Forbes's life and then of Sarah's, she has now come into her full inheritance. The shaping of the story—the storyteller's "prejudice"—is now hers to imagine, to flesh out, to set down for readers to absorb into the narratives of their own lives.

Surprising Reversals in "The Migraine Workers"

"Has Anybody Seen Miss Dora Dean?" is the last of the stories in *Miss Muriel* written from the perspective of the pharmacist's daughter. The collection's two other stories set in and around Wheeling deal with conflicts that the sheltered pharmacist's daughter would probably not have known first-hand. Ironically, it is Ann Petry—herself a pharmacist's daughter—who opens the door to these alternative perspectives. In assuming the viewpoint of Pedro Gonzales, the frustrated truck stop owner of "The Migraine Workers," and Charles Woodruff, the anguished high school teacher of "The Witness," she further probes the relationships making up the outwardly calm, inwardly seething community of Wheeling.

"The Migraine Workers" is a story about prejudices based on class, race, and physical size. The protagonist, Pedro Gonzales, is a big, fat man who feels defensive about his occupational status. Owner of "the best-known truck stop between New York and Buffalo" (113), he fiercely resents the breezy young out-of-towners he must serve. His angry ruminations about their hairstyles and clothing indicate that a generation gap separates him from his alleged adversaries. But his problems with his young customers have as much to do with class as with age. At the same time that he judges their character on the basis of their clothing and haircuts, he feels that they are making an unfair social distinction in their judgment of him. In his furious recollection of a glamorous young white woman whose pet ocelot lunged at him, for instance, he assumes that she saw him as "the big slob working twelve hours a day" (116). Because the woman's laughter has enraged him, he recklessly tells the police that "if she'd stayed long enough, I would have smashed her face in with the tire iron" (116). Although his business depends on his patrons, Pedro does not like being patronized; when his customers do not conform to his social mores, he lashes out against them. He prefers not to be reminded that his livelihood depends on his customers, who do not owe him anything besides the sum of their bills.

Despite his social hardship, Pedro can still be kind to people who are worse off than he is. He takes pity on a truckload of black migrants—whom his employee Mike comically misidentifies as "migraine workers" (117)—when their driver asks whether his human cargo might use the truck stop's rest rooms. Pedro is so horrified by the outright squalor of their existence that he provides all of them, including one especially pathetic old man, with a hearty meal as well as bathroom privileges.

His benevolence does not, however, prevent Pedro from viewing the migrants as a regrettable intrusion on his own tenuous peace of mind. His awareness of their misery is quickly supplanted by the comfort he takes in a routine day of work: "The trucks came and went and the drivers drank coffee and the regular customers came in for gas and oil and there weren't any ragged, hungry people who traveled standing up in rattletrap trucks or any blondes in convertibles with what looked like Bengal tigers on the seat beside them" (120). To him, the migrants and the obnoxious young woman all threaten his security. Pedro is no more able to solve the oppressed migrants' problems than he is to solve his own problems with the woman or any of "these rich kids" who seem to think they are better than he is (116). In the middle of a pecking order based on race and class, he is above the impoverished migrants but far below the rich white woman who laughed at him. Giving the migrants a large meal is an act of kindness, but it is also an act of charity, a measure of Pedro's higher status.

Just as he passes judgment on his customers, so do Pedro's social inferiors pass judgment on him. Ben, the ragged old migrant who furtively returns to Pedro's station, does not see Pedro solely as a kindly benefactor but rather as a "fat white man" who will have plenty of food to spare (125). Although Pedro would prefer to turn the vagrant over to the police, Mike convinces him that the old man should be allowed to stay. Mike explains Ben's crafty thinking: "Didn't you hear him say if he hadn't jumped off the truck when he did, he couldn't 'a found the *fat* white man's place?" (125). Unable or unwilling to refute Mike's logic, Pedro feels "betrayed by his own soft flesh" (125). Like the old black man, Pedro has been judged on the basis of his skin. His obesity has caused the old man to steal from him, just as the migrants' skin color had predicated their sorry state of degradation, a state that had influenced Pedro's earlier act of goodwill. Because Pedro had seen the migrants as the objects of his generosity, he had never imagined that, in their eyes, he, too, was an object.

Blind Injustice in "The Witness"

In both subject matter and tone, "The Witness" is by far the bleakest of the Wheeling stories. First published in *Redbook* in 1971, the story depicts Wheeling at a chilling juncture in the late 1960s or early 1970s. In the midst of an era when American women and minorities are demanding equal rights, the town's most intellectually promising white boys exhibit an appalling hatred of others, especially blacks and women. Their older peers seem depressingly bland and apolitical in their ambitions, but the sophomore class includes boys who are as incorrigible as they are intelligent. The story pits Woodruff, a widower still struggling with his loss, against these violent boys whose cruelty drives Woodruff from town.

Woodruff is an outsider to Wheeling. A college teacher from Virginia, he could not sustain interest in his retirement projects after his wife's death. He comes to Wheeling, to teach high school, as a means of assuaging his loneliness and grief. His late wife is still very much in his mind, however, and his recollections of Addie conjure up a disciplined, rather censorious woman—a type familiar to readers who remember Abbie from *The Narrows*. Like the highly image-conscious Abbie, Addie had urged her husband to wear the clothes and eyeglasses she deemed appropriate for a well-respected black man. Since her death, Woodruff has indulged himself in an expensive overcoat and a big car—and he cannot quite forgive himself for making such luxurious purchases. He is caught between the carefully crafted image his wife had wanted him to project during their life together and the image that has emerged after her death: "thinnish, tallish black man, clipped moustache, expensive (extravagantly expensive, outrageously expensive, unjustifiably expensive) overcoat, felt hat like a Homburg, eyeglasses glittering in the moonlight, feet stamping in the moonlight, mouth muttering in the moonlight" (213). Like the young narrator of "The New Mirror," Woodruff imagines the way his white community sees a black man. He assumes, as she does, that the description would inevitably suggest wrongdoing, no matter what the actual circumstances. Even though he is merely talking to himself outside the local Congregational church, he feels implicated, guilty of being different from the rest of the town's citizens. He does not fit comfortably into Wheeling, despite the community's praise for his teaching.

The young hoodlums, whom Woodruff helps the Congregational minister counsel, are quick to exploit Woodruff's insecurities. Because

Woodruff would know and fear the racist stereotype of a black rapist ter-
rorizing white women, they seize on him as a means of covering up their
gang rape of a young white woman. Although he catches them right as
they prepare to abduct the girl, the boys refuse to take the defensive. In
their eyes, Woodruff is "pro-tec-shun,"—a useful "ho-daddy" rather
than an intimidating figure of authority (222). The fine clothes and car
that represent Woodruff's assimilation into the white community
become weapons that the boys use against him. They steal the car, tie
him up in his coat, and break his glasses (thus symbolically crushing his
orderly vision of society).

The bound and blindfolded Woodruff does not technically "witness"
Nellie's rape in an isolated cemetery shed, but he can well imagine her
fate. When the boys finally force him to touch her half-nude body, he
sees a girl who "looked as though she were dead" (226). The boys remain
smugly confident that Woodruff will not turn them in. Anticipating his
fear of being framed, they respond to his muted pleas on the girl's behalf
by declaring: "You're our witness, ho-daddy. You're our big fat witness"
(227). The slang term denigrates Woodruff as a pimp, while the label
"witness" resonates with irony. The boys know Woodruff through the
church, where Woodruff and the pompous, ineffectual minister, serving
as "witnesses" for Christ, have attempted to indoctrinate them into the
ways of Christianity. Furthermore, while one might expect Woodruff to
serve as a legal witness helping to prosecute the boys, they see him as
their witness, a black man too fearful to do anything other than protect
them from exposure.

Like Lutie Johnson, Woodruff realizes that there is no safe place for
him in his community. Like Lutie, furthermore, he acts rashly to protect
himself. He is convinced that the boys will accuse him of the rape if he
reports what happened. Because he does not expect fair treatment from
anybody, he leaves town and thus avoids the moral issues at hand. Just
as Lutie leaves her young son to fend for himself, so Woodruff leaves
Nellie. He is trapped on one side by the boys' misogyny and racism and,
on the other, by his conviction that a black man's word will not be
believed. It is possible that he would be believed—and that the minister,
among others, would vouch for his honor—but Woodruff is afraid to
take the risk. None of his wife's careful crafting of his image can stop
him from condemning himself as "A witness. Another poor scared black
bastard who was a witness" (234). Perhaps worst of all, Woodruff is a
witness who will never tell his tale. As readers, we witness his fear and
shame and imagine the terrible aftermath of his silence.

Circles of Prejudice and Possibility

Through the course of the five Wheeling stories, Petry shows characters tormented by questions of race, gender, and identity. Significantly, the stories' protagonists—the pharmacist's daughter, the Hispanic truck stop owner, the high school teacher—are not just victims of prejudice; they are perpetrators of it. Although they revile the judgments passed by others, they are quick to jump to their own conclusions. Their notions about color, gender, age, and social class strongly influence their own actions. As a result, their dealings with others reflect a distinct lack of objectivity. This lack of objectivity makes them human and the community where they live realistic.

Their relationships in the Wheeling stories resonate far beyond their immediate significance to the characters involved. The Layen family, the Forbes family, Pedro and Ben, Woodruff and the high school punks all engage in private battles that have public, political dimensions. Although these characters do not see their struggles in a social context, Petry urges us to take a broader, longer view of their troubles, which are hardly peculiar to the citizens of Wheeling. In the range of the stories, their subtle interconnections, and their shifting time frame, Petry shows how the identity of a town—or a nation, for that matter—depends on one's point of view. Petry's multiple perspectives give Wheeling a depth and poignance that her characters rarely perceive. Reading about the town from many different angles, we can see both its endurance and its ability to adapt to (or at least withstand) the ways of new generations. Ironically and perhaps inevitably, the citizens of Wheeling dwell on their own limitations rather than their potential for growth and change.

Chapter Seven

Harlem and Beyond: The Perils of Thwarted Communication

In Ann Petry's fiction, prejudice alone does not always alienate people from each other. Often, a breakdown in communication combines with prejudice to polarize couples, families, and communities. The racial and sexual bias that Lutie Johnson experiences, for instance, leads her to believe that she cannot trust anyone. Once she is convinced that she has no viable relationships left in Harlem, she abandons her son and leaves the city forever. Her oppressed circumstances may be the catalyst for her dilemma, but her inability, or unwillingness, to communicate finally drives her into self-imposed exile from her family and community. Similarly, miscommunication derails Link's relationship with Camilla in *The Narrows*. Unable to overcome their stereotypes of each other, they allow half-articulated prejudices to supplant their love.

Thwarted communication is a conceit running through Petry's *Miss Muriel and Other Stories* as well. In different ways, "The Necessary Knocking on the Door," "Like a Winding Sheet," and "In Darkness and Confusion" all exemplify the dramatic consequences of suppressed communication. In each story, the protagonist's disinclination to express anger and frustration harms his or her relationships and eventually leads to catastrophe. The ramifications of blocked communication ultimately reinforce the destructive powers of prejudice.

Locked Minds in "The Necessary Knocking on the Door"

Set at a Christian women's conference, "The Necessary Knocking on the Door" (1947) has the quality of a biblical parable. In this nine-page story, the shortest in *Miss Muriel,* the relationship between a black woman and a white woman—or, more precisely, the *lack* of a relationship—symbolizes both the profound division between the races and the equally profound interdependence of the two.

Alice Knight, a black woman from Washington, D.C., has come to the conference in the Berkshires to commune with women who share her spiritual values. That all the other women are white does not stop her from attending the conference or participating in it with great satisfaction. But her pleasant illusion of acceptance is quickly, and irredeemably, destroyed at breakfast one morning by a fellow conferee. In response to a friendly overture from Alice, the white-haired Mrs. Taylor responds: "I've never eaten with a nigger and I'm too old to begin now" (247). Although the other women sitting with Alice had been discussing "minority groups in Europe" before Mrs. Taylor's comment (246), they are unable to confront a minority issue in their midst. The resulting breakdown in communication renders the high-minded "Annual August Conference on Christianity in the Modern World" a failure and a sham (245).

The breakdown takes the form of "a long, uneasy silence" followed by "a babble of conversation—bright, quick talk hastily assembled to fill up the hollow place made by the silence" (247). The white women's nervous desire to cover their own embarrassment does not alleviate the anger and hurt that Alice feels. On the contrary, the vapid chatter only makes her feel worse. Alice imagines that the women are "hurrying to build a bridge across the gaping silence. Each one of them is approaching with a straw to help build the bridge" (247). The flimsy, useless bridge of their conversation does nothing to erase Mrs. Taylor's cruel invective: "Why should a word, a two-syllable word, make me hate them? Not just that one white-haired white woman, but all of these others, too" (247). Mrs. Taylor's use of the word "nigger" thus succeeds in infuriating Alice as well as alienating her from all of the women. When the other women begin to babble, Alice turns silent, watchful, defensive, and bitter.

Alice's reactions to the incident at the breakfast table are so powerful, in fact, that she cannot bring herself to help Mrs. Taylor once the older woman falls ill. Responding to coughs and moans coming from the room across the hall, Alice gets up in the middle of the night to investigate. But once she realizes it is Mrs. Taylor making the desperate, inarticulate cries for help, she suspends her rescue mission. Her earlier encounter with Mrs. Taylor has convinced her that any overture on her part will be met with disparaging comments and suspicious inquiries. Rather than risk further damage to her dignity, Alice stops short of knocking on the sick woman's door.

The "necessary" knocking might well have prevented an unnecessary death: Alice learns the next morning that Mrs. Taylor died from a heart attack during the night. Worse, a maid tells her that "Doctor say if anybody'd known about her havin' a heart attack they coulda saved her" (251). A vengeful God seems to have brought his hand down on Mrs. Taylor, whose death so closely follows her openly expressed bigotry. But Alice Knight seems implicated as well. Her inability to turn the other cheek, to offer help to an adversary, exposes her own turpitude. The price of ignoring Mrs. Taylor's moans is a deep feeling of guilt; even before she knows that her nemesis is dead, Alice dreams of running away as a voice calls to her: "Yours is the greater crime. A crime. A very great crime" (250).

If "The Necessary Knocking on the Door" were not written from Alice's perspective, the story might seem to be an object lesson about prejudice: The mean old white woman dies as a result of her racist comment to a young, innocent black woman. But Alice's thoughts complicate the apparent moral of the story. We are aware of her anger and frustration, and we know that she chooses silence for much the same reason that the white women choose mindless banter: She does not want to confront prejudice head-on; she does not want to risk the dangers that come with any kind of involvement.

Nevertheless, by remaining silent, Alice becomes not only the victim of racism but also its tool. Her inability even to knock in response to Mrs. Taylor's wordless cries—let alone open the door and offer help— reveals the extent to which prejudice manipulates her life. She is incapable of the knocking, or communicating, that holds a community together. In this story, ignoring a cry for help presages death for the community as well as death for Mrs. Taylor.

Cyclical Abuse in "Like a Winding Sheet"

Whereas "The Necessary Knocking on the Door" deals with racial conflict between two women, "Like a Winding Sheet" addresses the impact of racism on a relationship between a black man and black woman. But here again, a white person's use of the word "nigger" causes a breakdown in communication. The black protagonist's response to the word represents a legacy of oppression as well as the anger of the moment, and that long history of thwarted communication continues to have disastrous ramifications.

Because Johnson, a Harlem resident and factory worker, has no satisfactory outlet for his suppressed rage, he finally does what he believes himself incapable of doing: He beats his wife. In a society that routinely strips minority citizens of their dignity, Johnson's unwillingness to hit a woman seems to be his sole point of honor. Yet his inability to express himself sufficiently in the face of discrimination, both real and imagined, finally pushes him over the edge. He takes out his frustrations on Mae because she has playfully called him "an old hungry nigger trying to act tough" (210); because she is an emblem of the other women who have enraged him that day; and, perhaps most important, simply because she is within striking distance when his silent fury finally explodes into brutal expression.

Like Alice Knight, Johnson realizes that he is trapped by his own inaction as much as by the racial oppression he must endure. The story is framed by the image of a winding sheet (traditionally used for wrapping a corpse) encasing Johnson as he struggles to cope with his suffocating life. In the opening scene, Mae gazes at Johnson in bed, reluctant to get up and go to his night-shift job, and observes humorously that he appears caught in a winding sheet. The image returns to Johnson's mind at the story's end when he cannot stop hitting his wife: "He had lost all control over his hands. And he groped for a phrase, a word, something to describe what this thing was like that was happening to him and he thought it was like being enmeshed in a winding sheet—that was it—like a winding sheet. And even as the thought formed in his mind, his hands reached for her face again and yet again" (210). Although Johnson is very much alive, he is oppressed to the point of being unable to act in any way that is not destructive. By striking Mae, he carries on the very tradition of oppression that he finds so despicable.

Johnson's attack on Mae is the more horrifying because it seems inevitable, the culmination of a series of frustrations gnawing at Johnson's powers of self-restraint. Four times in the course of the story, we learn that Johnson is not the type of man to hit a woman. The repeated assertion suggests that the possibility is much on his mind, however. When his wife's protestations about working on Friday the thirteenth make him late for work, he passes up the day's first opportunity to invoke violence: "He had to talk persuasively, urging her gently, and it took time. But he couldn't bring himself to talk to her roughly or threaten to strike her like a lot of men might have done. He wasn't made that way" (200). The second opportunity arises at the plant, when his female supervisor ridicules him for arriving late and refuses to accept his excuse about his aching legs: "And the niggers is the worse. I don't care what's wrong with your legs. You get in here on time. I'm sick of you niggers" (202). Although he reminds himself that "he couldn't bring himself to hit a woman" (203), neither his retort to his boss nor his physically threatening movement toward her quenches his desire to feel "the soft flesh of her face give under the hardness of his hands" (203). By this point, his desire to hit the woman seems to equal his desire to hold himself back: "A woman couldn't hit back the same way a man did. But it would have been a deeply satisfying thing to have cracked her narrow lips wide open with just one blow, beautifully timed and with all his weight in back of it. That way he would have gotten rid of all the energy and tension his anger had created in him" (204). Without any other outlet for his anger, he begins to fantasize about the satisfactions of hurting someone. But it is cold comfort in the face of the drudgery of his job, the pain in his legs, the exhaustion of working nights, and the knowledge that none of his good ideas for the plant will ever be implemented.

Johnson's frustrations continue to grow on his way home from work. When a white girl declines to serve him coffee, he assumes that her decision is based on race. The narrator informs us, however, that this incident is a matter of an empty coffee urn rather than blatant racism. Oblivious to the real circumstances, Johnson seethes with anger. His suppressed desire to hit a woman washes over him yet again. It seems that no matter where he turns, a woman is waiting to test the boundaries of his temper. As the day progresses, his determined refusal to hit a woman evolves into an uncontrollable desire to do just that. Perceiving himself as a victim of injustice, he finally indulges in victimization himself, only to find that becoming a tormentor does not ease his pain and frustration at all. As his closing thoughts indicate, he is horrified by his attack on Mae, the terrible fruition of his long torturous silence.

Cries of Anguish: "In Darkness and Confusion"

"In Darkness and Confusion" (1947) is the longest and most complex of these three stories dealing with blocked communication. Whereas "The Necessary Knocking" and "Like a Winding Sheet" both use single relationships as emblems for social ills, this novella places an entire family in the context of a deeply troubled, racist society. Written from the perspective of William Jones, a black janitor for a New York City pharmacy, the story takes an inside look at a World War II–era riot in Harlem. The difficulties experienced by William, his wife Pink, their son, Sam, and their niece Annie May are representative of the bottled-up desperation and anger that all the rioters feel. In addition, William's inability to communicate clearly symbolizes the entire black community's self-enforced silencing. When all of Harlem finally explodes in violent protest against a white police officer's killing of a black soldier, we can see that the riot is the furious, ultimately ineffectual voice of many long-silenced individuals like William.

William's difficulty with communication is evident from the story's beginning. Despite his obsessive thoughts about his wife, son, and niece, he is unable to articulate to any of them either his love or the fears he feels in their behalf. This problem fills him with frustration and creates barriers between him and his family.

The more he thinks about his son Sam, for instance, the less he is able to talk about him or communicate with him. It is only after a long silence from Sam, a soldier stationed in Georgia, that William musters the courage to write a letter: "He had sat and thought a long time. Then he wrote: 'Is you all right? Your Pa.' It was the best he could do. He licked the envelope and addressed it with the feeling that Sam would understand" (259). The letter compresses all of William's anxiety and love for his son into a brief, ungrammatical inquiry. Although his vivid memories of Sam's youth and his high hopes for his son reveal the extent of his preoccupation with Sam, William does not convey any of this in his letter. He has little experience writing letters "because Pink had always done it for him" (259), and the prospect of giving voice to his feelings nearly overwhelms him. The sheet of paper before him is "blank and challenging" (259), and he grips his pencil so hard that his hand is drenched in sweat. Writing the letter, let alone mailing it, is a huge act of courage for William. It is also a huge risk, for the act of asking a question places William in the vulnerable position of awaiting his son's response. His horror at Sam's silence can only increase, the longer his laboriously written missive goes unanswered.

William's communication problems are equally apparent in his truncated conversations with his wife and niece. There is an enormous gap between his extensive thoughts about Pink and Annie May and his brief exchanges with them. Because his infrequent attempts at communication have routinely met with anguish or hostility, he has come to rely increasingly on silence as a means of keeping the peace. Once he realizes that Pink dreads being asked whether a letter from Sam has arrived, William internalizes all of his anxiety about his son. He does not tell Pink that he has written a letter to Sam. Instead, he assumes his own private vigil over the mailbox, in hopes of discovering the much-desired letter himself.

Once William and Pink stop talking to each other about their son, a fissure opens up between them. William assumes that the question of Sam's fate is his alone to resolve. He does not see that confiding in Pink might make it easier for him to bear the terrible news; instead, he grows increasingly alienated from Pink at the same time that he is eaten up with horror and fear. By pretending to be asleep when she comes home from work, by staying in bed the next morning until she is nearly ready to leave for church, and by commenting on the weather rather than bringing up more pressing subjects, William believes he is protecting his wife from news she would be unable to bear. Unfortunately, his silence only exacerbates his own suffering and deprives Pink of information she has a right to know.

William's relationship with Annie May is also characterized by blocked communication. He is disgusted by his eighteen-year-old niece's refusal to hold a steady job and by the late hours she has begun keeping. Afraid that she might be tempted into prostitution, he tries without success to chastise and discipline her. In their exchanges, he comes off as a bully; she seems like a petulant child. They are further alienated from each other by Pink, who dotes on her orphaned niece and derails William's attempts at discipline. For all of his concern about Annie May's education and well-being, then, William is perceived by both Annie May and Pink as an obtuse adversary.

Annie May's high school principal is a more likely candidate for that role. The principal, "a large-bosomed white woman," declares Annie May "a slow learner" and evidently has no interest in keeping her in school (265). William's inability to express himself prevents him from defending his niece, whom he knows to be intelligent. In this instance, both he and Annie May are defeated by his silence: "Before he knew it he was out in the street, conscious only that he'd lost a whole afternoon's pay and he never had got to say what he'd come for. And he was boiling mad with himself. All he'd wanted was to ask the principal to help him persuade Annie May to finish school. But he'd never got the words together" (265).

William is far from alone in his communication difficulties. In addition to Pink and Annie May, who also suppress many of their thoughts and feelings, the black men he socializes with at the local barbershop are just as reluctant as William to talk about important matters. It is in the barbershop that William finally learns his son's fate: Scummy, a soldier who knows Sam, tells him that Sam has been sentenced to twenty years of hard labor for shooting a white military policeman. According to

Scummy, Sam refused to sit in the back of a bus; the officer shot him; Sam then shot the officer. The revelation momentarily silences everybody in the barbershop. As in "The Necessary Knocking on the Door," when the white women respond to a racist remark first with silence and then with a babble of conversation, the men in the barbershop eventually pick up their usual patter of conversation.

The men in the barbershop seem to follow a script of "safe" conversation. Before his conversation with Scummy, William himself had been parroting white people's views of the Japanese: "Most every time he started talking about the Japs the others listened with deep respect. Because he knew more about them than the other customers. Pink worked for some navy people and she told him what they said" (267). Neither William nor any of the other men can articulate their feelings about racism. A pervasive presence in all of their lives, it plagues them collectively and individually. Because they don't talk about its impact on them, it also alienates them from one another. Their frustrations are the worse for being suffered in isolation.

The riot that occurs after a white police officer guns down a black soldier creates the illusion of shared purpose among the blacks of Harlem. William, for his part, welcomes the opportunity to unleash his pent-up fury. The shooting he has witnessed seems to be an uncanny replication of the wrong suffered by his son. Swept up in the emotion of the angry crowd, he feels his individual identity slipping away: "It frightened him at first. Then he began to feel powerful. He was surrounded by hundreds of people like himself. They were all together. They could do anything" (282). The solidarity of the crowd even gives him the strength to tell Pink about Sam's fate after he bumps into her on the street. When Pink's sorrow takes the form of violence—she screams and hurls a bottle through a store window—he welcomes the spontaneous release of tension: "The violent, explosive sound fed the sense of power in him. Pink had started this. He was proud of her, for she had shown herself to be a fit mate for a man of his type" (287). Ironically, it is only in his identification with the mob that William seems to have acquired any stature in his own eyes. Just as he feels that the very existence of the unruly throng somehow speaks for him, so does he also seem to feel that Pink's incendiary act gives voice to the convictions of the throng.

The ensuing riot connects the personal tragedy borne by William and Pink with the unjust killing that has outraged the crowd. For William, the death of the anonymous soldier readily symbolizes the loss of his son. It seems possible that everybody in the throng brings a similarly personal experience of injustice to this public expression of racially motivated outrage. The riot represents a host of long-stifled voices speaking as one.

But the voice of the mob is essentially a cacophony of chaos. The vandalism, looting, and arson incited by Pink's hurled bottle do not presage harmony among Harlem's blacks, but rather expose the dissonance characteristic of the larger community of both blacks and whites. The rioters' seemingly powerful actions are, more precisely, pathetic reactions to an institutionalized racism far beyond their control. That they believe, even for a moment, that smashing property and looting businesses will even the score suggests the terrible depth of their oppression. Moreover, their ruinous rampage plays right into the hands of their oppressors: Having briefly run amok, they will be corralled by the police, punished, and effectively silenced once again. Much like Johnson's attack on his wife in "Like a Winding Sheet," the riot represents the eruption of jumbled, painful emotions. Hardly a solution or a call for justice, the riot is, instead, a further manifestation of a vast problem. The community is so divided by racism that peaceable communication between the races no longer seems possible.

Panic quickly supplants William's vicarious experience of power. Once he realizes that his fellow rioters are being arrested, he begins to see the mob for what it is: a singularly desperate and disorganized response to injustice. With the return of his individual conscience comes the conviction that he must gather together his family and move beyond the horror of the moment. But his conviction comes too late: too late for him to help Sam, imprisoned for the next twenty years; too late to tell Annie May, who has been arrested, that he now understands her unwillingness to conform to a culture that regards her as expendable; and too late for him to comfort Pink, whose superhuman assault on a liquor store's locked gates drains the last of her strength. Now that Pink's lifeless body lies at his feet, his voice is a cry in an unheeding wilderness:

> All his life, moments of despair and frustration had left him speechless—strangled by the words that rose in his throat. This time the words poured out.
>
> He sent his voice raging into the darkness and the awful confusion of noises. "The sons of bitches," he shouted. "The sons of bitches." (295)

Now that he has lost Sam to a labor camp, Annie May to the police, and Pink to death, his isolation is complete. All of the people most likely to listen to him are gone. His furious, unfocused invective has nowhere to go but into the pandemonium of the night. Like his letter to Sam, William's anguished shouts will go unanswered.

Self-Expression in "Olaf and His Girlfriend" and "Solo on the Drums"

The theme of thwarted communication does not always spell doom in Petry's short fiction. In "Olaf and His Girlfriend," for example, the long separation of the West Indian Olaf from his beloved Belle Rose does not end their relationship. Although their communication is blocked by Belle Rose's disapproving aunt, a thread of contact is preserved by the sailors who pass on word to Olaf of Belle Rose's whereabouts in New York. When he discovers her singing West Indian voodoo songs in a nightclub, he is quick to step forward and claim her as his own. Their communication has been thwarted but not aborted.

Likewise, in "Solo on the Drums," blocked communication does not lead to disaster. Abandoned by his wife for another man, the drummer Kid Jones channels all of his sorrow and frustration into his stage performance. Ironically, he must perform side by side with the pianist with whom his wife has fallen in love. Like Sonny in James Baldwin's story "Sonny's Blues," Kid Jones has a viable outlet for feelings that might otherwise go unexpressed. Thanks to his musical talent, he is far from silent, and the voice of his solo rises above his individual experience and moves everybody who hears him play.

Neither of these two stories is directly concerned with racial prejudice. Without the catalyst of racism, communication problems in Petry's fiction seem more controllable, less likely to take on tragic proportions.

The Communication of Bias, the Bias of Communication

In "The Necessary Knocking on the Door," "Like a Winding Sheet," and "In Darkness and Confusion," all of the protagonists are subjected to racism. Their problems seem to hinge on a belief that verbal communication, far from solving their troubles, may make their situations even worse. Alice Knight cannot bring herself to speak to Mrs. Taylor or obtain help for her for fear of being further insulted by the white women at the Christian conference. Johnson breaks down and beats his wife because he does not know how else to express his rage at being branded a "nigger." And William Jones suppresses his need to communicate for so long that he finally loses all the family members he most wants to address. Overwhelmed by racism and undercut by self-doubt, all three characters find themselves trapped in a netherworld somewhere between speech and silence. Their plights speak vividly to us, even as these tortured figures resist the urgent need to speak for themselves.

Chapter Eight

A Statue, a Skeleton, an Imaginary Friend: Stories of Projected Identity

Confused identities have long provided a rich theme for writers of romantic comedies. With its pansy-dust potions, Shakespeare's *A Midsummer Night's Dream* suggests that love is literally in the eye of the beholder. Even as we laugh at the befuddled lovers, the play also asks us to question our own perceptions of what is real and what is imagined. Ann Petry likewise mines this vein, though not always with comic intent: In *The Narrows*, Link Williams and Camilla Sheffield initially mistake each other's racial identities. They compound their initial errors by imposing racial and gender-based stereotypes on each other, and their love affair ends in Link's death rather than the blissful nuptials characteristic of Shakespearean comedy. In "Mother Africa," "The Bones of Louella Brown," and "Doby's Gone," Petry also explores the theme of confused—or, more precisely, projected—identities. These stories show how the identities that one projects on others often reveal much more about oneself than the objects of one's interest.

Changing Faces in "Mother Africa"

In "Mother Africa" (1971) Harlem junk dealer Emanuel Turner experiences an identity crisis at the same time that he conjures up a fanciful identity for a statue. A fiercely independent man who holds white people in low regard, he reluctantly accepts the bronze statue of a nude woman, the cast-off of a wealthy Long Island widow. Appalled by the statue's imposing size and nudity, Man (as his friends call him) believes the windfall "just went to prove how a white woman would trick a black man every time—even one she'd never seen" (134). His customers' reactions confirm his suspicion that the statue will be an embarrassment as well as a nuisance: Women are scandalized by the statue's brazen appearance, while men laugh and gawk as if it were a stripper inviting their appraisal.

Despite his initial reaction and the reactions of his customers, Man gradually falls under the spell of the dark-colored statue he comes to thinks of as "Mother Africa" (139). To honor and protect his new acquisition, he decides to clean up his ramshackle junkyard and improve his disheveled appearance. His transformation appears to be a direct response to the statue, which reminds him of his late wife. After she died in childbirth, he had been desolate until he stumbled on the haphazard freedoms of the junk business. As "Rags, Ole Rags, Junk, Ole Junk, Bottles, Ole Bottles" (127), Man has had a safe, well-defined role in his Harlem neighborhood. It is only the presence of the magnificent nude that calls that role into question.

Like his customers, Man views the statue as a gendered entity rather than an inanimate work of art. But Man's response to the statue is more complicated than his neighbors' burlesque humor. His nickname "Man" perhaps reflecting a universal male bias, he regards the statue as if it were a living woman. Thus he reverses the courtly love tradition of treating an unattainable woman as if she were a goddess sculpted on a pedestal. The statue's color precipitates his reverence as much as her voluptuous features do. He sees her as an emblem of both racial pride and female beauty. As "Mother Africa," the statue becomes the motivating presence in Man's life.

Changing his identifying features—his hair, smell, and clothing—to match the statue's grace and beauty sparks a terrible identity crisis within him. He has unwittingly shed his carefree existence along with his beard and dirty clothes. Before, his slovenly appearance had assured him a comfortable identity as a man whose way of life suited the way he looked. Once the object of mild amusement and disdain, he has now reclaimed outward respectability, but the neighborhood children "stared at him distrustfully, as though suddenly confronted by a stranger who had not yet declared whether he was friend or foe" (159). And the statue no longer provides either solace or inspiration: "She was only a statue, made of some dark metal. Yet he resented her as deeply as though she had been a live woman who had tricked him into cutting off his beard" (158). Worst of all, "He kept wondering whether he had done the best possible thing with his life, whether perhaps he'd missed his original destiny" (159). Even though it seems as if the statue has taken over his life, his real dilemma stems from free will: Despite his long-standing habits, he is fully capable of change. He need not be exactly what the children or his customers expect him to be.

Man's final revelation about the statue exposes flaws in his judgment while simultaneously illuminating his plight. Having scrutinized the statue's facial features, he realizes: "He'd been so busy looking at her breasts and her thighs, he hadn't paid any attention to her face. Besides, bronze darkened with age and just on the basis of the darkness of the metal, he had thought this was a statue of a shapely black woman" (161). The shock of his miscalculation causes him to tumble off a ladder and injure himself. This literal fall into knowledge leaves Man humiliated and angry. But his knowledge is incomplete, since he does not connect his own experience with the statue's. Though he has just suffered the indignity of the children's puzzled stares, he does not grasp the ways that other people's perceptions inevitably determine and objectify one's identity.

Like the children, Man conflates identity with identifying features. Once he views the statue as a white woman, he considers it tangible proof of his original suspicion that a white woman is always trying to trick a black man. Ironically, the statue really *is* an object with no free will of its own, so Man's perceptions—along with those of the anonymous pranksters who attempt to cover it up—fully determine its identity and status in the community.

Man's desire to be rid of the statue, and all of its troubling associations, recalls the reason he received it in the first place: The Long Island woman gave it up because her husband had a heart attack and died in an attempt to move it. The statue, then, is already an emblem of misfortune. The white woman considers it the agent of her husband's death, while Man considers it proof of a white woman's trickery. In either case, the statue embodies whatever its beholders project on it. Its size and representation of female nudity provide the basis for all sorts of imaginative interpretations of its meaning.

The end of the story, when Man calls the Harlem Metalworks, reveals the statue's impact on his life:

> He said he had a large bronze statue. About ten feet. He was selling her for scrap. Yes, he had the papers on her.
> "Come right away," he shouted. "Hurry." (162)

The use of the feminine pronoun suggests that Man still sees the statue as a female entity even as he sells it as scrap metal. For him, the statue's problematic nature arises from its representations of gender and race and his responses to those representations. The statue brings his troubled

thoughts to mind. But disposing of the statue will not clear up the conflicts he feels about race relations and male-female relations. He is in
effect killing the messenger because he knows no other way to deal with
his embarrassment and disgust. Although the story does not tell us what
the future holds for him, it seems unlikely that Man will continue his
one-man crusade for order and cleanliness. Without "Mother Africa"
towering over his home, he will have lost the vision and the motivation
necessary to change his life.

The Body Politic in "The Bones of Louella Brown"

Although "Mother Africa" has its lighthearted moments, "The Bones of
Louella Brown" (1947) is by far the most humorous story in *Miss Muriel*.
Through parodic characterizations and a consistently arch tone, it sati-
rizes the importance people place on race and social status, among other
outwardly defining characteristics.

Set in Boston, the story concerns a mix-up involving the disinterred
skeletons of a black washerwoman and a prominent white woman,
Elizabeth Bedford, also known as the Countess of Castro. The highly
publicized confusion scandalizes Whiffle and Peabody, the elderly white
undertakers handling the disinterment. Hired by Governor Bedford, a
Boston patriarch intent on moving all of his deceased kin to the newly
constructed Bedford Abbey, Whiffle and Peabody have complicated
matters by also disinterring the body of Louella Brown, a laundress who
worked for Peabody's mother. Her burial in the exclusive Yew Tree
Cemetery has long troubled Peabody, who believes that a black woman
has no place in a "white" burial ground. The disinterment of the
Bedfords presents Peabody with the opportunity to quietly remove
Louella's body as well.

A complication arises in the form of Stuart Reynolds, an ambitious
Harvard medical student working for Whiffle and Peabody. Fascinated
by the similarities between the skeletons of the laundress and the
countess, Reynolds calls up the *Boston Record* with his exciting revelation. A crafty newspaper editor then distracts Reynolds so that no one
can tell which skeleton is which. Thus Reynolds thoroughly embar-
rasses himself and his employers. The story quickly becomes international news: "As the twenty-first of June approached, people in New
York and London and Paris and Moscow asked each other the same
question: Who would be buried in Bedford Abbey, the countess or the
laundress?" (172).

As in many of her other works, Petry indicates in this story that blacks are not the only ones who bear the brunt of prejudice. While Whiffle believes that nothing could be worse than confusing a Bedford with a black washerwoman, Peabody offers a larger—that is, even more broadly biased—perspective:

> "She might have been Irish," said Old Peabody coldly. He was annoyed to find how very clearly he could see Louella. With each passing day her presence became sharper, more strongly felt. "And a Catholic. That would have been equally as bad. No, it would have been worse. Because the Catholics would have insisted on a mass, in Bedford Abbey, of all places! Or she might have been a foreigner—a—a—Russian. Or, God forbid, a Jew!" (171–72)

Neither man realizes the absurdity of the situation, nor does the elderly Governor Bedford, who sharply reprimands the two for the trouble they have caused. Though their distress is comical, the story makes a serious point: Prejudices regarding race, creed, and color may reflect human nature, but there is no underlying logic to back them up. Death, the great equalizer, renders one skeleton pretty much the same as the next.

The spirit of Louella Brown plays a viable role in the story. Laughing and full of the vibrancy Peabody remembers from his childhood, she is the projection of the elderly undertaker's guilty feelings. Her amusement marks the foolishness of the dilemma at hand, while her presence reminds Peabody that she was a good, strong-minded woman, not a mere supplicant. Goaded by Louella's laughing spirit, Peabody finally convinces Governor Bedford to acknowledge both the laundress and the countess in the family crypt. The inscription, "HERE LIES ELIZABETH, COUNTESS OF CASTRO OR LOUELLA BROWN, GENTLEWOMAN 1830–1902" (180), suggests the interchangeability of the two skeletons, while according dignity to both women. The even-handed wording does not reflect Peabody's and Bedford's mature judgment so much as it does their latent guilt and fear. While Bedford contemplates the undertaker's suggestion, he has "the uneasy feeling that he could already hear Louella's laughter" (180).

The vision of a laughing black woman is finally poignant, since Louella Brown would have had scant opportunity to influence white male power brokers in her lifetime. It is Bedford's fear of dying, not a newly awakened sense of social justice, that causes him to acknowledge the washerwoman's life and death. Peabody plays on this fear to relieve his own terror: "He is afraid to die, Old Peabody thought, eyeing the Governor. You can always tell by the look on their faces. He shrugged his shoulders. 'Every man dies alone, Governor,' he said brutally. 'And so it is always best to be at peace with this world and any other world that follows it, when one dies'" (179).

But even though their motivations are selfish, the recognition Louella Brown receives in the Bedford crypt is a victory. Long after Peabody and Bedford have expired, the marble text equating the laundress and the countess will remain. The placement of the inscription at the end of "The Bones of Louella Brown" underscores the epitaph's finality as well as its implicit irony.

Realities of Friendship in "Doby's Gone"

In "Doby's Gone" the theme of confused identity takes yet another form. Here, a young girl enrolling in first grade must confront both racial prejudice and peer pressure for the first time. New to the town of Wessex, Connecticut, Sue Johnson has an imaginary friend, Doby, with whom she prepares for the first day of school. Because she has grown up in a rural area without friends her own age, her parents have not discouraged her fantasy. But when her new classmates begin to torment her, Sue finds that Doby is no help.

Until she enters first grade in Wessex, Sue defines herself largely in terms of her relationship with Doby. She imagines that he is always present, accompanying her on train rides, joining her for meals, playfully plucking ribbons from her hair. Entering the new world of the school yard only strengthens her faith in their inviolable friendship: "She held on to Doby's hand a little more tightly. Now she was actually going to walk up that long gravel walk to the school. She and Doby would play there every day when school was out" (299). It is only when other children surround Sue during recess that her fantasy world is called into question. At first, she merely retreats from the white children's racist insults. Her bewilderment takes the form of tears and whispered comfort for Doby: "'Don't you mind. I won't let them hurt you'" (301). Later, she tells her concerned mother that she runs home from school because "'Doby doesn't like the other children very much'" (303). As yet unable to acknowledge relationships with her peers, she filters her emotions through the always amicable Doby. Projecting her feelings onto him enables her to express herself without revealing her loneliness and vulnerability.

Physical contact with the other children literally jolts Sue out of her fantasy world. When they begin to pull her hair and push her, she must respond to them directly, without Doby as intermediary: "While she was slapping and kicking at the small figures that encircled her she became aware that Doby had gone. For the first time in her life he had left her. He had gone when she started to fight" (303–4). Her new self-reliance earns her the other children's respect, and, in the aftermath of the fight, Sue spends the afternoon playing with two new friends, Daisy Bell and Jimmie. The shift from imaginary to real friends is swift and irrevocable.

But when she finally goes home, Sue wavers between two worlds as she tries to remember what she has lost. She regresses for a moment when her worried mother asks her what is wrong: "'Oh,' she wailed, 'Doby's gone. I can't find him anywhere'" (305). Now that real friends have materialized, she no longer needs Doby. Her sorrow is a poignant reminder of the pain involved in growing up. But the transition brings new joys along with new responsibilities. Though Daisy Bell and Jimmie lack Doby's unflagging equilibrium, they will provide Sue with the contact and the context necessary to develop her identity and find a niche of her own.

"Doby's Gone" is a fitting ending to *Miss Muriel and Other Stories*, since all of the collection's characters are, in effect, imaginary friends through whose eyes we see several communities and numerous relationships. Although these characters do not understand just how interconnected their lives are, Petry's rounded portrayals of them enable us to draw conclusions that they overlook. Throughout *Miss Muriel*, Petry's creations struggle to differentiate themselves even as they reveal an innate kinship through all of their words and deeds.

Chapter Nine

Petry's Legacy

In the course of a half century, Ann Petry has created a host of memorable characters. Thanks to her attention to detail and her refusal to pass snap judgments on anyone, they are believable as well as memorable. The depth and breadth of characterization in *The Street, Country Place, The Narrows* and *Miss Muriel and Other Stories* go a long way toward explaining the emotional charge that all of Petry's works carry. While society marginalizes many of the people that she brings to life, in her pages they take center stage and demand our serious consideration. The stories of their lives demand, furthermore, that we look at them in context: the contexts of their relationships, their communities, and their place in American society. Petry's portrayal of them requires us to acknowledge the interdependence that they, for a multitude of reasons, cannot or will not see.

Although Lutie Johnson's life is central to *The Street,* we come away from that novel understanding Mrs. Hedges, Jones, Min, Boots Smith, Miss Rinner, and even Junto in addition to Lutie and her son Bub. Likewise, we depart *Country Place* intimately familiar with Doc and the Weasel but also well acquainted with the Roane family, the Gramby family, and the infamous Ed Barrell. Completing *The Narrows,* Petry's most expansive rendering of a community, we know not only Link Williams but also nearly everybody who has ever been important to him: Abbie Crunch, Bill Hod, Weak Knees, Frances Jackson, Camilla Treadway Sheffield, and Jubine, among many others. And, after our sojourns in *Miss Muriel*'s Wheeling and Harlem, among other places, we cannot do justice to Mr. Bemish without describing Sophronia's other two suitors; we cannot characterize John Forbes without discussing his widow and the acquaintances permanently affected by his suicide; we cannot talk about William Jones without explaining Pink, Annie May, and Sam.

We cannot isolate Petry's characters from one another, because we do not apprehend them that way. We see them interacting with family members, neighbors, coworkers, acquaintances, and strangers, and those interactions are the essence of their lives and stories.

Yet Petry's characters do not always recognize—or recognize in time—the extent to which their lives are connected. Alice Knight cannot bring herself to knock on Mrs. Taylor's door. Glory Roane does not foresee the disastrous effects of kissing Ed Barrell on Obit's Heights. Malcolm Powther does not imagine the fatal ramifications of pointing out Link Williams to Bunny Sheffield and Mrs. Treadway. William Jones does not know that telling Pink about Sam's fate will precipitate a riot and bring on her death. Boots Smith does not anticipate the consequences of forcing himself on Lutie. Again and again, Petry's characters assume they are acting alone when they are actually part of a large ensemble cast. Often at odds with their communities, they fail to realize that their own choices help determine the character of the towns they revile.

Their inability to change their lives for the better or to see their lives in context frequently leads to anger, despair, and violence. Each of the three novels ends in sudden, violent death: Boots Smith, Ed Barrell and Mrs. Gramby, and Link Williams do not survive the telling of their tales. In *Miss Muriel,* we encounter the deaths of Pink Jones, John Forbes, Sarah Forbes, and Mrs. Taylor, whereas images of death permeate most of the other stories.

The frequent physical abuse that characters inflict on each other further represents their pervasive state of anguish. Johnson's sudden attack on his wife, Link's angry grapplings with Camilla, and even Lutie's slapping of her son are all misguided expressions of deep-seated frustration. Their feelings of racial and sexual oppression find temporary release in these attacks, but the violence itself only perpetuates the cycle of oppression, frustration, fury, and abuse.

The recurring theme of self-imposed exile reveals feelings of disaffection and alienation among Petry's characters. Following in Lutie Johnson's wake, Johnnie Roane, Mr. Bemish, and Charles Woodruff all leave their communities suddenly, convinced that exile is their only viable option. They are willing to forsake their families, homes, jobs, or a combination thereof, because they would rather vanish into the unknown than remain in a place where they feel disenfranchised.

Even in situations that do not end in open warfare or expulsion, Petry's characters often pull away from each other, sacrificing intimacy even as they accept the facts of coexistence. The narrator of "The New Mirror" realizes that she and her family have internalized the racial prejudices that objectify them in the community's eyes. Accepting this, she tacitly withdraws from her family while explicitly withdrawing from the white townspeople. A similar kind of distancing occurs in *Country Place,* where Mrs. Gramby, her son Mearns, and his wife Lil communicate indirectly and often coldly, despite their familial ties. Only Portulacca, Mrs. Gramby's Portuguese gardener, is able to thaw the icy atmosphere and reach out to Neola, the usually standoffish black maid (the rehabilitated ghost of Lutie Johnson) who accepts his marriage proposal.

Communion within Community

On first reading—or even second or third reading—Petry's fictional communities may appear overwhelmingly sad. There are so many angry characters, so few saving acts of generosity and love. We might even wonder whether Abbie Crunch's seemingly selfless decision to aid Camilla is her way of evening the score with Bill Hod. In novel after novel, story after story, the American dream is a time bomb exploding in vulnerable hands. Illusions of a better life torment those who realize, with appalling clarity, that their lives are only getting worse.

But in Petry's communities, people do not live in isolation, no matter how alienated they feel. Alienation itself is an inherently socialized emotion, since the truly alienated person would not know what he was missing. Even *The Street*'s Jones, a pathologically alienated figure, mourns the loss of intimacy in his life. He feels its absence with every cell of his being. Jones, Lutie, Miss Rinner, Johnnie Roane, Alice Knight, and Charles Woodruff are too preoccupied with the injustices they have suffered to comprehend either the interconnectedness of their relationships or the centrality of those relationships to the communities they occupy.

Alienation emerges, finally, as the most crushing illusion of all. The real pathos of Petry's works lies in her characters' inability to see what is readily apparent to us: Individuals do not act or react in a vacuum. Their decisions, their shortcomings, their finger-pointing, their threats, blows, and occasional acts of courage and grace all determine the community's form and future. People live intrinsically social lives, and their smallest movements have repercussions far beyond their conception.

Coming away from Petry's fictional communities, we can look over and beyond the limits that her characters so often impose on themselves. We can recognize the curative power of friendship demonstrated by Mrs. Hedges's assisting Min and Mrs. Gramby's leaving her home to her servants. But we must also acknowledge that individual acts of generosity are far from a panacea: The sexism, racism, and other prejudices that Petry depicts cannot be easily vanquished. The 116th Street tenements are still with us, after all; they are not just nightmare images in a 1946 novel.

Despite all the despair, the anger, the cold winds, storms, and concealing fogs in Petry's fiction, her overall portrait of community life contains an undeniable element of hope. Petry's decision to write about seemingly unexceptional, sometimes undesirable, people imbues their lives with value and meaning. Her willingness to take up William Jones's perspective, Min's, and Malcolm Powther's tells us that these are people worth knowing, worth thinking about. No matter how little they think of themselves, these characters are there, on the page, for us to probe and ponder.

The act of storytelling is itself an eminently hopeful act. Stories passed down from generation to generation, books passed from one reader to another, and anecdotes embroidered with each retelling are all a means of connecting with others, ensuring a sense of communion that transcends the literal boundaries of any one community. Petry's abiding interest in the relationships between tellers and their tales, made explicit in "Has Anybody Seen Miss Dora Dean?" and *Country Place,* informs all her works. Her experimentation with a variety of narrative techniques, especially multiple points of view, illustrates her devotion to the art of writing.

The legacy Petry leaves us is as multidimensional as the communities she creates. We can read her stories and novels as testimony to the connectedness of individual lives, relationships, and communities. We can interpret her characters' travails as object lessons, paths to avoid. We can accept characters like Lutie, Mrs. Hedges, Doc, the Weasel, Abbie, Charles Woodruff, and Emanuel Turner for what they are: flawed, fallible witnesses of their times. And as critics, we can explore Petry's work from many angles. Her novels and stories cry out for narratological dissection, feminist critiques, New Historical approaches.

The legacy that Petry leaves younger black women writers has already begun to take tangible shape. Authors as diverse as Toni Morrison, Alice Walker, and Gloria Naylor have built on Petry's concept of the community and the relationships that hold it together. Morrison's *Song of Solomon* (1977), Walker's *The Color Purple* (1982), and Naylor's *The Women of Brewster Place* (1982) are among those works that show how much potential the community offers its fictional residents and its creators.

Naylor has paid tribute to Petry's importance to her and, by extension, to all black women writers in need of powerful role models. In her speech honoring Petry in November 1992, Naylor said,

When I, coming up twenty years later, from the time [*The Street*] is set, went to capture that same neighborhood, I turned toward another facet of that diamond, another facet of that truth. . . . [L]ooking at women who are first fighting battles within themselves, battles within their homes, within their own community, and ultimately with the community they would come in contact with, I had wanted to write about the transcendence of those forces, the other part of that diamond, the women who somehow managed to believe, who refused to be beaten down. . . . Because the Harlem that I knew was the Harlem of hope.[1]

For Naylor, *The Street* provided both a point of departure and a counterpoint for her own portrait of Harlem. In *The Women of Brewster Place,* she demonstrates her desire to follow in Petry's footsteps while broadening the creative path.

Petry's vision of community, though always acknowledging prejudice and violence, is essentially a liberating one. Her commitment to exploring and understanding many different points of view invites us to do the same, as readers, writers, and members of our own communities.

Notes and References

Chapter One

1. Arna Bontemps, "The Line," *Saturday Review of Literature,* 22 August 1953, 11.

2. Ann Petry, "Ann Petry," in *Contemporary American Autobiography Series* 6 (Detroit: Gale Press, 1988), 253–69; hereafter cited in text as *CAAS*.

3. Ann Petry, "The Novel as Social Criticism," in *The Writer's Book,* ed. Helen Hull (New York: Harper and Brothers, 1950), 35.

4. Ann Petry quoted in Esther B. Fein, "An Author's Look at 1940's Harlem Is Being Reissued," *New York Times,* 8 January 1992, B1; hereafter cited in text.

5. Ann Petry quoted in David Streitfeld, "Petry's Brew: Laughter and Fury," *Washington Post,* 25 February 1992, E2; hereafter cited in text.

6. Sybil Weir, "*The Narrows:* A Black New England Novel," *Studies in American Fiction* 15, no. 1 (Spring 1987): 88; hereafter cited in text.

7. Angela Y. Davis, *Women, Race, and Class* (New York: Vintage Books, 1983), 98; hereafter cited in text.

8. Petry's first published story ("Marie of the Cabin Club," *Afro-American,* 19 August 1939, 14), a brief work crammed with action and romance, appeared under the male pseudonym Arnold Petri. Although this story largely enabled Petry to break into print as a fiction writer, it is in "On Saturday the Siren Sounds at Noon" that her thematic concerns first emerge.

9. Ann Petry, "On Saturday the Siren Sounds at Noon." *Crisis* 50 (December 1943): 369; hereafter cited in text as "On Saturday."

10. Richard Wright, *Native Son* (New York: Vintage Books, 1972), xxvii.

11. Marjorie Green, "Ann Petry Planned to Write," *Opportunity: Journal of Negro Life* 24, no. 2 (April–June 1946): 78.

12. James Ivy, "Ann Petry Talks about First Novel," *Crisis* 53, no. 2 (February 1946): 48.

13. "First Novel," *Ebony,* April 1946, 36; hereafter cited in text as "First Novel."

14. James Ivy, "Mrs. Petry's Harlem," *Crisis* 53, no. 5 (May 1946): 48; hereafter cited in text.

15. Roger William Riis, "A Story of 'Hemmed In' Lives," *Opportunity: Journal of Negro Life* 24, no. 3 (July–September 1946): 157.

16. Ann Petry, *The Drugstore Cat* (Boston: Beacon Press, 1988), 87.

17. "About the Author," jacket copy for Ann Petry's *Harriet Tubman: Conductor on the Underground Railroad* (New York: Crowell, 1955).

18.   Ann Petry, "The Common Ground," in *Horn Book Reflections,* ed. Elinor W. Field (Boston: Horn Book, 1969), 71–72; hereafter cited in text as "Common Ground."

19.   Hazel Ervin, "Just a Few Questions More, Mrs. Petry," in *Ann Petry: A Bio-Bibliography* (New York: G. K. Hall and Co., 1993), 102.

20.   Ann Petry, "The Moses Project," *Harbor Review,* no. 5–6 (1986): 52–61.

Chapter Two

1.   Community also plays an important role in Petry's books for young adults, *Tituba of Salem Village* (1964) and *Harriet Tubman: Conductor on the Underground Railroad* (1955), and one of her two books for children, *The Drugstore Cat* (1949). This study focuses on Petry's books for adult readers.

2.   Although the word "community" is now commonly used to designate minority solidarity crossing geographic boundaries—for instance, "black community" and "gay community"—I do not use these connotations here. For the purposes of this study, the term "community" denotes a specific, geographically definable city, town, or neighborhood where specific people live.

3.   Asked whether she considered herself a member of "the naturalistic school of writing," Petry replied, "I always want to do something different from what I have done before; I don't want to repeat myself. If I belong to a certain tradition, I don't want to belong, because my writing would be very boring if I always wrote in a particular style" (John O'Brien, "Ann Petry," in *Interviews with Black Writers* [New York: Liveright, 1973], 160; hereafter cited in text.)

4.   For Petry's account of her life, see *CAAS.*

5.   Ann Petry, "Harlem," *Holiday* 5, no. 4 (April 1949): 164; hereafter cited in text as "Harlem."

6.   Ann Petry, *The Street* (Boston: Beacon Press, 1985), 57–58; hereafter cited in text.

7.   Barbara Christian, *Black Women Novelists* (Westport, Conn.: Greenwood Press, 1980), 64; hereafter cited in text.

8.   Ann Petry, *Miss Muriel and Other Stories* (Boston: Beacon Press, 1989), 210; hereafter cited in text as *Miss Muriel.*

9.   Petry's pointed reference to the beautiful street in Lyme suggests a subtle irony in the novel's title: *The Street* may refer to the street in Lyme, where Lutie's naive pursuit of the American dream begins in earnest, as well as 116th Street, where her thwarted hopes devolve into rage and homicide.

10.   Roger Rosenblatt, *Black Fiction* (Cambridge: Harvard University Press, 1974), 139.

11.   Ann Petry, *Country Place* (Chatham, N.J.: Chatham Bookseller, 1971), 3; hereafter cited in text as *CP.*

12.   The Narrows, as an enclave existing within a larger community, is akin to Petry's "shameful and unjustifiable" Harlem set down in the midst of New York City.

13. Ann Petry, *The Narrows* (Boston: Beacon Press, 1988), 415; hereafter cited in text as *Narrows.*

14. Vernon E. Lattin, "Ann Petry and the American Dream," *Black American Literature Forum* 12, no. 2 (Summer 1978): 71.

15. Gladys J. Washington, "A World Made Cunningly: A Closer Look at Ann Petry's Short Fiction," *CLA Journal* 30, no. 1 (September 1986): 18–19.

16. For Petry's publications in periodicals, see Ervin's *Ann Petry: A Bio-Bibliography.*

Chapter Three

1. Keith Clark, "A Distaff Dream Deferred? Ann Petry and the Art of Subversion," *African American Review* 26, no. 3 (1992): 503.

2. Toni Morrison, *Playing in the Dark: Whiteness and the Literary Imagination* (Cambridge: Harvard University Press, 1992), 35.

3. Marjorie Pryse, "'Pattern against the Sky': Deism and Motherhood in Ann Petry's *The Street,*" in *Conjuring: Black Women, Fiction, and Literary Tradition,* ed. Marjorie Pryse and Hortense J. Spillers (Bloomington: Indiana University Press, 1985), 125–26.

4. In a 1973 interview, Petry says, "*The Street* was built around a story in a newspaper, a small item occupying perhaps an inch of space. It concerned the superintendent of an apartment house in Harlem who taught an eight-year-old boy to steal letters from mail boxes" (O'Brien, 160).

5. Given Lutie's admiration for Benjamin Franklin, it is ironic that Junto's name evokes her role model and hero. Marjorie Pryse points out that "the name *Junto* is . . . a direct allusion to the first significant men's club in American colonial history, the name Franklin gave his secret group of friends" (Pryse, 118).

6. Nellie Y. McKay, "Ann Petry's *The Street* and *The Narrows*: A Study of the Influence of Class, Race, and Gender on Afro-American Women's Lives," in *Women and War: The Changing Status of American Women from the 1930s to the 1950s,* ed. Maria Diedrich and Dorothea Fischer-Hornung (New York: Berg, 1990), 135.

7. Michael G. Cooke, *Afro-American Literature in the Twentieth Century: The Achievement of Intimacy* (New Haven: Yale University Press, 1984), 39.

Chapter Four

1. Wallace Stevens, "The Noble Rider and the Sound of Words," in *The Necessary Angel: Essays on Reality and Imagination* (New York: Vintage Books, 1951), 33. Petry and Stevens (also a Connecticut resident, living in Hartford) were simultaneously mulling over the relationship between reality and imagination. In 1947, the year *Country Place* appeared, Stevens published *Transport to Summer,* which includes "Credences of Summer" and "Notes toward a Supreme Fiction," two long poems concerned with the "interdependence" he describes in his essay.

2.   Vernon E. Lattin, "Ann Petry and the American Dream," *Black American Literature Forum* 12 (1978): 71.

Chapter 5

1. Margaret McDowell, *"The Narrows:* A Fuller View of Ann Petry," *Black American Literature Forum* 14 (1980): 136.

2.   Along the same line of interpretation, Vernon E. Lattin argues for significance in the newspaper editor's name: "As his name suggests, Bullock is the castrated American male. A white man who has sold his freedom to search for wealth, he is the typical twentieth-century American male" (Lattin, 71).

3.   Only a comma separates Link's indoctrination into religion from the "awful business" of sex. It seems that Abbie and Frances are not much more comfortable discussing spiritual concerns than matters of the flesh.

Chapter 6

1.   Mr. Bemish addresses Sophronia as "girlie" when he proposes marriage to her (45). We may wonder just how lucid the shoemaker is: Has he inhaled glue fumes for so long that he cannot remember his beloved's name? Or does he, like the narrator's father, view Sophronia as a child?

Chapter 9

1.   Gloria Naylor, "Tribute to Ann Petry," Ann Petry Conference, 14 November 1992, Trinity College, Hartford, Connecticut.

Selected Bibliography

This bibliography lists all major publications of Ann Petry's work and selected secondary works.

PRIMARY WORKS

Novels

Country Place. Boston: Houghton Mifflin, 1947. Reprint, London: Michael Joseph, Ltd., 1948. Reprint, Chatham, N.J.: The Chatham Bookseller, 1971. Foreign reprint. *Tempeste.* Translated by V. E. Bravetta. Roma: Jandi Sapi, 1949. Aided and abetted by the town taxi driver, pharmacist "Doc" Fraser recounts the domestic upheavals occurring during the space of a week in Lennox, Connecticut. The town's troubles climax during a terrible storm. In this second novel, Petry writes almost exclusively about white characters.

The Narrows. Boston: Houghton Mifflin, 1953. Reprint, London: Gollancz, 1954. Reprint, New York: Signet, 1955. Reprint, London: Ace Books, 1961. Reprint, New York: Pyramid, 1971. Reprint, Boston: Beacon Press, 1988. Link Williams, a young black man, falls in love with a beautiful white heiress whose family controls the city of Monmouth, Connecticut. Their love affair exposes the many problems polarizing the city and its black community known as the Narrows.

The Street. Boston: Houghton Mifflin, 1946. Reprint, New York: Pyramid, 1946, 1961. Reprint, London: Michael Joseph, 1947. Reprint, New York: Signet, 1947. Reprint, Boston: Beacon Press, 1985. Reissue, Boston: Houghton Mifflin, 1992. Also translated into numerous foreign languages, including Dutch, French, German, and Japanese. Lutie Johnson is a young black woman striving to provide her son with a safe home in Harlem. She battles oppression on all fronts, as do all of her acquaintances in her impoverished neighborhood.

Collected Short Fiction

Miss Muriel and Other Stories. Boston: Houghton Mifflin, 1971. Reprint, Boston: Beacon Press, 1989. This first collection of short fiction by an African-American woman compiles stories Petry wrote from the 1940s through 1971. Several of the stories are set in Wheeling, New York, a small town similar to Petry's native Old Saybrook, Connecticut. Others are set in Harlem, drawing on the decade during which Petry lived in New York City.

Uncollected Short Fiction

"Marie of the Cabin Club." *(Baltimore) Afro-American,* 19 August 1939, 14.
(Published under the pseudonym Arnold Petri.) This melodramatic short
short story packs murder and romance into a single page.
"The Moses Project." *Harbor Review* 5–6 (1986): 52–61. The black male protagonist under house arrest manages to outsmart the electronic device
monitoring his whereabouts.
"On Saturday the Siren Sounds at Noon." *Crisis* 50 (December 1943): 368–69.
Before jumping to his death, a black man recalls the death of his child in
a fire and his revengeful murder of his wife.

Children's Fiction

The Drugstore Cat. Illustrated by Susanne Suba. New York: Crowell, 1949.
Reprint, Boston: Beacon Press, 1988. Buzzy, a temperamental kitten,
discovers the pleasures of human companionship at the James Pharmacy.

Children's Nonfiction

Harriet Tubman: Conductor on the Underground Railroad. New York: Crowell,
1955. Reprint, New York: Washington Square, 1971. Also published as
The Girl Called Moses: A Story Biography of Harriet Tubman. Illustrated by
Judith Valentine. London: Methuen, 1960. Also appears in *Braille Book
for Juvenile Readers.* Washington, D.C.: Library of Congress, 1960.
Foreign reprint. *Het Leven van Harriet Tubman.* Translated by
Geschiedenis Voor Jenge Mensen. Amsterdam: C. P. J. Van der Peet. In
a compelling style appropriate to adult readers as well as younger ones,
this biography tells the life story of the courageous woman who helped
many of her fellow blacks escape the oppression of slavery during the
Civil War.
Legends of the Saints. Illustrated by Anne Rockwell. New York: Crowell, 1970.
In vivid language, Petry provides biographical sketches of saints.
Tituba of Salem Village. New York: Crowell, 1964. Reprint, New York: Harper,
1988. Recorded. Division for the Blind. Washington, D.C.: Library of
Congress, 1964. This narrative chronicles the life of the black slave
woman from Barbados who was tried as a witch in eighteenth-century
Salem, Massachusetts.

Poetry

"Noo York City 1." "Noo York City 2." "Noo York City 3." *Weid: The
Sensibility Revue* (Bicentennial Issue II, American Women Poets) 12, nos.
45, 46, 47 (December 1976): 125–27. With Petry's characteristic clarity
of voice, the poems in this sequence create a three-panel portrait of urban
life. A black laundryman and a dying black woman take center stage.

"A Purely Black Stone." In *A View from the Top of the Mountain,* edited by Tom
    Koontz and Thom Tammaro, 75. Daleville, Ind.: Barnwood Press
    Cooperative, 1981. The title refers to the headstone to be placed on the
    grave of Mr. Ed, a laundry proprietor beloved by his employees.
"A Real Boss Black Cat." In *A View from the Top of the Mountain,* edited by Tom
    Koontz and Thom Tammaro, 76. Daleville, Ind.: Barnwood Press
    Cooperative, 1981. Using slang characteristic of the 1960s, this poem's
    speaker expresses his desires and ambitions.

Autobiography

"Ann Petry." In *Contemporary Authors Autobiography Series,* edited by Adele
    Sarkissian, 6: 253–69. Detroit: Gale Research, 1988. Petry recalls her
    family origins, her childhood in Old Saybrook, the defining moments in
    her development as a writer.
"My Most Humiliating Jim Crow Experience." *Negro Digest,* June 1946, 63–64.
    At age seven Petry attended a Sunday school picnic at a public beach.
    Because of her race, the whole group was made to leave.

Screenplay

That Hill Girl. Hollywood, Calif.: Columbia Pictures, 1958. Petry was invited
    to write this script as a vehicle for Kim Novak.

Nonfiction

"The Common Ground." In *Horn Book Reflections,* edited by Elinor Whitney
    Field, 67–72. Boston: Horn Book, 1969. In an anecdotal style, Petry dis-
    cusses the importance of writing books about interesting, memorable
    characters to provide young readers, especially black children, with com-
    pelling role models.
"The Great Secret." *Writer* 61, no. 7 (July 1948): 215–17. Drawing on her
    experience as a writer, Petry cites the importance of understanding
    human nature and mastering the craft of storytelling.
"Harlem." *Holiday* 5, no. 4 (April 1949): 110–16, 163–66, 168. A lengthy arti-
    cle, with photos, describing the arts, culture, landmarks, and society life of
    Harlem as well as the community's poor housing and pervasive poverty.
"The Lighter Side." *People's Voice,* 7 March 1942–8 May 1943. In this weekly
    column Petry recorded arts and society news and witty anecdotes from
    the Harlem community.
"New England's John Henry." *Negro Digest* 3, no. 5 (March 1945): 71–73.
"The Novel as Social Criticism," In *The Writer's Book,* edited by Helen Hull,
    32–39. New York: Harper, 1950. Petry argues that literature and social
    criticism need not be mutually exclusive.

"Tribute to Mr. Gentry." *Connecticut Pharmacist* 3 (November 1946): 5, 42. A salute to pharmacists, as embodied by the fictionalized Mr. Gentry.

"Tubman, Harriet." *Encyclopedia Britannica.* 1970, 22: 302. A brief sketch of the black slave who helped other slaves escape to freedom in the North.

"What's Wrong with Negro Men?" *Negro Digest,* March 1947, 4–7. A satirical attack on the appearance and attitudes of black men.

SECONDARY WORKS

Adams, George R. "Riot as Ritual: Ann Petry's 'In Darkness and Confusion.'" *Negro American Literature Forum* 6 (1972): 54–57, 60. Suggests that the riot in "In Darkness and Confusion" provides protagonist William with an archetypal rebirth.

Bell, Bernard W. *The Afro-American Novel and Its Tradition.* Amherst: University of Massachusetts Press, 1987. Reprint, 1989. Argues that Petry explores literary territory beyond naturalism and exposes the inconsistencies within the mythologies of African-American life and culture.

———. "Ann Petry's Demythologizing of American Culture and Afro-American Character." In *Conjuring: Black Women, Fiction, and Literary Tradition,* edited by Marjorie Pryse and Hortense J. Spillers, 105–15. Bloomington: Indiana University Press, 1985. Writes that Petry, in an improvement over Chester Himes and Charles Wright, realistically locates her fictional black communities in geographical, historical, and cultural contexts.

Bell, Roseann P., Bettye J. Parker, and Beverly Guy-Sheftall, eds. *Sturdy Black Bridges: Visions of Black Women in Literature.* New York: Anchor Press, 1979. Cites Petry's importance to a younger generation of African-American women writers.

Bone, Robert. *The Negro Novel in America.* New Haven: Yale University Press, 1965. Praises *Country Place* for its characterization and style, while labeling *The Street* an "environmentalist" novel in debt to Richard Wright's *Native Son.*

Brown, Thomasine Corbett. "Elements of Naturalism in Ann Petry's *The Street.*" Master's thesis, University of North Carolina at Chapel Hill, 1966. Through an analysis of plot, point of view, setting, characters, and theme, Brown argues the novel's use of naturalism.

Christian, Barbara. *Black Women Novelists: The Development of a Tradition, 1892–1976.* Westport, Conn.: Greenwood Press, 1980. Places *The Street* in the context of other novels by African-Americans and discusses Lutie Johnson's inability to find the emotional support she needs in the communities where she lives.

Clark, Keith. "A Distaff Dream Deferred? Ann Petry and the Art of Subversion." *African American Review* 26, no. 3 (1992): 495–505. Analyzes the rhetorical effect of the multiple narrative perspectives Petry uses in *The Street.*

Condon, Garret. "Street Wise: The Rediscovery of Ann Petry and Her Timeless Stories of the Cruel City." *Northeast.* Sunday supplement of the *Hartford Courant,* 8 November 1992, 8, 13, 18–20. Feature story about Petry's life and writings.

Davis, Arthur P. *From the Dark Tower: Afro-American Writers 1900 to 1960.* Washington, D.C.: Howard University Press, 1974. Analyzes *The Street, Country Place, The Narrows,* and *Miss Muriel and Other Stories,* reserving praise for *Miss Muriel.*

Dempsey, David. "Uncle Tom's Ghost and the Literary Abolitionists." *Antioch Review* 6 (1946): 442–48. Criticizes the violent ending of *The Street* but praises Petry for developing complex black characters.

Ervin, Hazel Arnett. *Ann Petry: A Bio-Bibliography.* New York: G. K. Hall and Co., 1993. This invaluable resource for Petry scholars contains an annotated bibliography of primary and secondary sources and a selection of six interviews with Petry.

———. "The Subversion of Cultural Ideology in Ann Petry's *The Street* and *Country Place.*" Ph.D. diss., Howard University, 1993. Addresses the feminist rhetoric underlying Petry's first two novels.

Fein, Esther. "Author's Look at Harlem of 40's to Be Reissued." *New York Times,* 8 January 1992, B1–2. Feature story about Petry and the reissuing of *The Street.*

"First Novel." *Ebony,* April 1946, 35–39. Richly detailed feature story about Petry's debut as a novelist and the success of *The Street.*

Gayle, Addison, Jr. *The Way of the New World: The Black Novel in America.* Garden City, N.Y.: Anchor/Doubleday, 1975. Discusses *The Street*'s multiple layers of meaning and rates the novel as superior to *Native Son.*

Greene, Marjorie. "Ann Petry Planned to Write." *Opportunity: Journal of Negro Life* 24, no. 2 (April–June 1946): 78–79. Biographical sketch of Petry, culminating with her Houghton Mifflin Fellowship Award.

Harris, Trudier. *From Mammies to Militants: Domestics in Black American Literature.* Philadelphia: Temple University Press, 1982. Describes Lutie Johnson's role as a domestic worker who, significantly, views her position as transitional rather than permanent.

Hernton, Calvin C. *The Sexual Mountain and Black Women Writers: Adventures in Sex, Literature, and Real Life.* New York: Anchor Press, 1987. Reprint, 1990. Praises *The Street*'s naturalism, social realism, and bold feminism.

Holladay, Hilary. "Creative Prejudice in Ann Petry's 'Miss Muriel.'" *Studies in Short Fiction* 31 (1994): 667–74. Argues that the social prejudices embodied by the suitors in "Miss Muriel" are creative forces rather than merely destructive ones.

———. "*The Street:* Lutie Johnson's Avenue of Escape." *South Carolina Review.* Forthcoming. Argues that in killing Boots Smith and leaving Harlem behind, Lutie may be seen as "a radical heroine" who at least temporarily stays the pervasive oppression of black women.

Hughes, Carl Milton. *The Negro Novelist: A Discussion of the Writings of American Negro Novelists, 1940–1950.* New York: Citadel Press, 1953. Reprint. 1970. Praises Petry's language and characterization in *Country Place.*

Isaacs, Diane Scharfeld. "Ann Petry's Life and Art: Piercing Stereotypes." Unpublished Ph.D. diss., Columbia University Teachers College, 1982. Thorough analysis of Petry's novels and stories, with a focus on the way Petry transcends stereotyping in her fictional characterizations.

Ivy, James. "Ann Petry Talks about Her First Novel." *Crisis* 53 (1946): 48–49. Interview with Petry at the time of *The Street*'s release. (Also collected in Ervin.)

Jones, Gayl. "Jazz/Blues Structure in Ann Petry's 'Solo on the Drums'." In *Liberating Voices: Oral Tradition in African American Literature.* Cambridge: Harvard Univ. Press, 1991, 90–98. Analyzes the "musical-literary form" of Petry's story.

———."Mrs. Petry's Harlem." *Crisis* 53 (1946): 154–55. Review of *The Street,* criticizing Petry's harsh portraits of Harlem life.

Lattin, Vernon E. "Ann Petry and the American Dream." *Black American Literature Forum.* 12 (1978): 69–72. Discusses the social criticism woven into Petry's fiction

McDowell, Margaret. "*The Narrows:* A Fuller View of Ann Petry." *Black American Literature Forum* 14, no. 4 (1980): 135–41. A close reading of the novel, with special attention to its use of alternating points of view and flashbacks.

McKay, Nellie Y. "Ann Petry's *The Street* and *The Narrows:* A Study of the Influence of Class, Race, and Gender on Afro-American Women's Lives. In *Women and War: The Changing Status of American Women from the 1930s to the 1950s,* edited by Maria Diedrich and Dorothea Fischer-Hornung, 127–40. New York: Berg, 1990. Analyzes the social biases informing the two novels from an African-American feminist perspective.

———.Introduction to *The Narrows.* Boston: Beacon Press, 1988. Discusses Petry's artistry in *The Street, Country Place,* and *The Narrows.* Cites opportunities for feminist criticism of *The Narrows,* which McKay considers Petry's most thoroughly developed novel.

Madden, David. "Ann Petry: 'The Witness.'" *Studies in Black American Literature* 6 (1975): 24–26. Analyzes the race and class biases exposed in Petry's story.

Maund, Alfred. "The Negro Novelist and the Contemporary Scene." *Chicago Jewish Forum* 12 (1954): 28–34. Compares Lutie Johnson with Wright's Bigger Thomas and analyzes *The Street* and *The Narrows.*

Mobley, Marilyn Sanders. "Ann Petry." In *African American Writers,* edited by Lea Baechler and A. Walton Litz, 347–59. New York: Charles Scribner's Sons, 1991. A well-written biographical essay, including literary analysis of Petry's works.

O'Brien, John, ed. "Ann Petry." In *Interviews with Black Writers,* 153–63. New York: Liveright, 1973. Interviews Petry about her approach to writing. (Also collected in Ervin.)

Pryse, Marjorie. "'Pattern against the Sky': Deism and Motherhood in Ann Petry's *The Street.*" In *Conjuring: Black Women, Fiction, and Literary Tradition,* edited by Marjorie Pryse and Hortense J. Spillers, 116–31. Bloomington: Indiana University Press, 1985. Discusses the "deistic" qualities of Petry's first novel, along with *The Street*'s implicit criticism of the black community's failings.

Riis, Roger William. "A Story of 'Hemmed in' Lives." *Opportunity* 24, no. 3 (Summer 1946): 157. Criticizes the unhappy fates doled out to characters in *The Street.*

Rosenblatt, Roger. "White Outside." *Black Fiction.* Cambridge: Harvard University Press, 1974. Praises *Country Place* as an example of a black novelist's creation of well-rounded white characters.

Shinn, Thelma J. "Women in the Novels of Ann Petry." *Critique* 16, no. 1 (1974): 110–20. A survey of Petry's female characters, including Lutie Johnson, Abbie Crunch, and Mamie Powther.

Streitfeld, David. "Retraced Steps on a Grim Street." *Washington Post,* 25 February 1992, E1–2. Interview with Petry and her daughter at the time of Houghton Mifflin's reissue of *The Street.*

Thomson, Rosemarie Garland. "Ann Petry's Mrs. Hedges and the Evil, One-Eyed Girl: A Feminist Exploration of the Physically Disabled Subject." *Women's Studies* 24, no. 6 (September 1995): 599–614. A character analysis of Mrs. Hedges, Lutie Johnson's neighbor in *The Street.* Focuses on Mrs. Hedges's positive aspects.

Washington, Gladys J. "A World Made Cunningly: A Closer Look at Ann Petry's Short Fiction." *CLA Journal* 30, no. 1 (September 1986): 14–29. A survey of Petry's *Miss Muriel and Other Stories,* discussing Petry's artistry and her realistic portrayals of African-Americans.

Washington, Mary Helen. *Invented Lives: Narratives of Black Women, 1860–1960.* New York: Doubleday, 1987. Praises the insider's perspective that Petry brings to small-town life in "Miss Muriel," while taking issue with the portraits of urban blacks in *The Street.*

Weir, Sybil. "*The Narrows:* A Black New England Novel." *Studies in American Fiction* 15, no. 1 (1987): 80–93. Examines Abbie Crunch's prototypical New England traits and places the novel in a continuum of works by New England authors.

Wilson, Mark K. "A *MELUS* Interview: Ann Petry—The New England Connection." *MELUS* 15, no. 2 (Summer 1988): 71–84. A delightful interview focusing on Petry's literary influences and the autobiographical sources for her fiction. (Also collected in Ervin.)

Index